THINKING OUT LOUD

ALSO BY MIKE HALL

Autumn's Back Porch: Reflections of a Life

THINKING OUT LOUD

Mike Hall

RESOURCE *Publications* · Eugene, Oregon

THINKING OUT LOUD

Resource Publications
An Imprint of Wipf and Stock Publishers
199 W. 8th Ave., Suite 3
Eugene, OR 97401

www.wipfandstock.com

PAPERBACK ISBN: 978-1-6667-4517-7
HARDCOVER ISBN: 978-1-6667-4518-4
EBOOK ISBN: 978-1-6667-4519-1

05/13/22

FOR LINDSAY, GRANT, AND WHITNEY

Thanks for all the precious memories you have given me

Contents

INTRODUCTION

This collection of poems is just what the title would indicate. It is me thinking out loud. They are spontaneous efforts, inspired by a variety of events – watching TV, conversations, observations, etc.

I began writing them on January 6, 2021, in response to the takeover of the Capitol Building. It was one of the lowest points in the history of our nation, an event which, for me, was frustrating to watch. The poems dealing with this singular event were my way of venting my disappointment in the participants, at how easily they were led to partake in the violence and mayhem that ensued during the course of that day.

I continued to write down my thoughts through the next days, weeks, and months.

The work grew into this collection. Each poem has a note at the end with a thought or observation about where my mind was at the time. As always, I want the poems to offer encouragement and hope during difficult times but also to give us a chance to pause and reflect upon the events happening in our own neighborhoods, cities, country, and world.

Mike Hall

THE POETIC VOICE

At times, the voice comes from the pit of despair,
    sounding out a hopeless message.
It can come from the weight of depression,
    burdened with anxieties too numerous to count.
Anger from abuse or neglect can spawn its call.
Frustration with societal grievances can add to its volume,
    increasing its timbre to a reverberating pitch.

Then at times . . .

It can reawaken times of happiness and joy,
    lifting the spirit to soaring heights
    or remind humanity of the blessings in evidence—
        nature's miracles,
        a child's laughter,
        love's healing power,
        kindness toward the unfortunate.
The voice can inspire, encourage, sway, and stimulate.

The voice causes us to pause, think, and question.
It is impactful in its use.
It has a message for each to hear.
It might be a whisper; it might be a roar,
    but it beckons to be heard.
It continually searches for its audience—
    sometimes large . . . sometimes small . . . but always present.
It will continue to thrive as long as humanity listens.

Note: This is my way of expressing why I have chosen to try my hand at writing poetry. It has been therapy for my soul since May of 2020 when the pandemic was really beginning to escalate. I have continued this effort during the year of 2021.

SEARCHING FOR WORDS

I am searching for the next idea,
the next set of words to pen,
something meaningful and worth reading.

I have waited a lifetime for the words to arrive,
for the ideas to pour forth onto the page,
for the words to be validated by others.

I am still scratching my head as I sit in my chair,
streamed music filling the quiet,
hopeful the lyrics might spark a thought.

I read other poets' offerings,
keeping my mind open for something to come knocking,
welcoming it to come in and have a chat.

I take a break and go for a walk outside.
I feel the sun on my face, a gentle breeze against my skin.
I look up and watch the clouds suspended, floating along in God's heaven.

I watch children playing in their respective yards,
running and laughing, seemingly carefree from worry,
unaware of society's troubles and struggles.

I see people walking and talking on their phone,
unable to separate . . . to disconnect . . . to take a break,
unwilling to press the pause button for just a little while.

I observe the mail truck driving along,
its driver unknowing if happiness or sadness is being delivered.
Maybe it will be a winning sweepstakes notice.

What about the butterfly I see fluttering along,
appearing weightless in the breeze I feel,
patiently exploring the flowers within its path.

Or the squirrel bounding across the street,
scaling a large oak effortlessly,
hurrying to its hidden home somewhere up high.

Oh well, it's time to head back to my chair and continue the search,
but I can be patient for the idea to arrive, for the words to come.
I don't want to settle for something that feels inadequate or superficial.

A good night's sleep might help.
Maybe sweet dreams will get the ball rolling,
for tomorrow will be another day to keep searching.

I pray I will be given another day to enjoy on this Earth,
a day to be thankful for all of God's blessings.
I know the words for which I am searching will eventually come.

Note: I have been reading the poetry of Billy Collins. It is like talking and reminiscing with an old friend. I am amazed at how his observations can make a point very discreetly and indirectly.

FIRE BURNING BRIGHT

The fire started small but grew,
consuming the material in the pile,
the brilliant yellows and oranges of the flames
reaching into the night sky,
sparks fluttering into the breeze feeding the fire.
People are standing and watching the blazing inferno,
the heat pushing them back, but still they persist in their vigil—
    captivated . . . mesmerized . . . enthralled by what they are witnessing.

The pages from the books burning in the pile are the perfect tinder;
the conflagration was hungry for more—
    the old pages igniting quickly, the flames licking up the welcome nourishment.
The crowd had gathered to see the destruction of the controversial texts,
to witness the symbolic wiping out of thoughts and ideas.
Within the crowd,
    some cheered,
    some stood numb,
    some cried,
    some asked the question, "Why?"

The book can be burned, but the words contained therein remain intact.
Words endure.
They take on a life of their own.
They might be attacked and punched constantly but somehow, withstand the barrage.
They keep coming back, round after round after round.
The stories, the thoughts, the ideas . . . they last.

The words find a permanent home—
    on the pages of the mind,
    on the pages of the heart.
How do you burn a mind or heart?
Only if humanity throws itself onto the pyre,
sacrificing its very soul.

Note: I began to dwell on the times during history when people have tried to censor thought by burning books which have been deemed controversial or which go against the established norm of mainstream society. It is an exercise in control.

THE RELEVANCE OF ONE

One—a single unit
Stick "l" on the front and you have "lone"
Lone—"the one," unique, to stand apart—
    the lone champion,
    the lone survivor,
    the Lone Ranger.
Type in an "a" to lead the way.
"Alone" is built on one,
    still meaning separate or apart,
    maybe even unequaled.
To be alone isn't necessarily undesirable—
    alone long enough to figure out who you are;
    alone long enough to figure out if you like yourself;
    alone long enough to contemplate and plan—
        learning to enjoy the quiet,
        learning to enjoy conversations with the person in the mirror.
Attach "-ly" on the end, and a new word is created;
emotions come into play with this new creation.
"Lonely"—not enjoying the aloneness or solitude—
    depressed from being the lone one,
    depressed from being separated,
    depressed from the lack of personal contact;
the need to share and belong is overwhelming.

Does "one" always have to deal with isolation and separation?

Don't like lonely?

Remove the "-ly" and attach "-ness."

Consider . . . oneness—

    sameness—coming together as one in thought;

    unity—common belief, aim, goal, faith . . .

        a slew of "one's" joining hand in hand,

        a slew of "one's" with strong conviction.

Remove the feeling of loneliness and become part of something greater.

Whether separate or joined by others,

    consider the relevance of "one,"

    consider the power of "one."

Note: I was exploring how the root or core of something can branch out into so many other things and take on so many other meanings.

MY FAITHFUL COMPANION

I stand watch over my domain,
a guardian . . . a sentinel . . . a protector,
waiting until she arrives to stand the next watch,
relieving me of my duties.
Ours is a devoted partnership built on trust—
never wavering . . . undaunted . . . constant.

I heard her arrive and came to attention,
eagerly anticipating her entrance,
filled with pride that I had successfully fulfilled my duty.
All was in order . . . all was quiet . . .
My laser-beam focus is aimed at the door
as it slowly swings open, and she steps through.

Our greeting ritual begins—
her grabbing my face in both hands, a scratch behind the ears, my bark of
welcome.
She changes clothes while I retrieve my leash.
It is time for me to lead her to the park
where we can run and play,
helping her to unwind before her duty begins.

I have worked with her for six years,
getting her in peak condition.
She throws the ball really well now,
and her frisbee skills are a little better than good.
There is still room for improvement,
but I must remember she is a work in progress.

I walk proudly by her side—my head held high—
showing her off to my other canine friends.
I am the envy of my pack.
I can tell by the way they look and stare,
by the way they wag their tail,
acknowledging our presence as we walk on.

She provides my meal right on time,
understanding consistency is important to her training.
We settle in for some time together talking and watching television.
I like the show where they run, chase, and kick the ball into the net.
The crowd gets really excited when this happens.
It would be even better if they included their dogs in the game.

It is time to call it a day.
I walk off to my bed to settle in,
waiting for sleep to overtake me,
where dreams of chasing rabbits await.
I draw comfort that she is on duty now.
She is now my guardian . . . my sentinel . . . my protector.

Note: My daughter and her husband are extremely devoted to their female chocolate Labrador they have named Maple. I thought it might be fun to look at their relationship from Maple's perspective.

TRULY LIVING

People are walking all around me,
breathing in and breathing out,
their respiratory system working as was intended,
supplying oxygen to all vital organs,
sustaining life as it was designed . . .
But is this living?
Is breathing to be equated with living life?
Are they chasing their dreams?
Are they loving others fully?
Are they practicing kindness?
Are they living a life for others to model?

I can't help but wonder how many are just making the day,
stuck in the same old routine, in an ever-deepening rut—
    mired in regret . . .
    mired in frustration . . .
    mired in complacency . . .
I realize that not everyone who is breathing is truly living.

Note: We are capable of so much more. Routine can provide comfort but can be a trap from which we are unwilling to escape.

I CAN DO WHAT I CAN

I want to do more
but doubt my best will be enough.
What difference will my effort make?
I fear others will belittle my contribution
because it seems so slight,
insignificant in its magnitude,
like a small ripple on a lake.

Should I just concede and let apathy hold sway?
Should I just continue on without a second thought?
just becoming one of the countless crowd,
embracing the comfort of the status quo.

But what if enough small contributions
combine to make one big whole.
Could my efforts be the beginning of something large?
Doesn't it have to start somewhere?
or . . . start with someone?

I can do what I can with what I have.
I can do what I can where I am.
I can do what I can, hoping it is the spark.
I can take the first step and do what I can.

Note: I ran across a quote made famous by Theodore Roosevelt who was quoting Squire Bill Widener: "Do what you can, with what you have, where you are." Roosevelt was a man of action, and his words call for us all to make our own contribution. It can be impactful on a small scale or maybe even much grander on a bigger stage.

OPEN DOORS

Walking down a long corridor—
      Doors open
      Doors close
      Go through? or hold back
Decisions to consider—
      What if the wrong door is chosen?
      What if the door closes because of indecision?
Too much thinking—
      Commit!
Walk through to experience what is on the other side—
      Can't watch from the outside
      Can't speculate
Learn from the experience
There will be other doors, other opportunities
When a door closes . . . He will open another
Be ready . . . be decisive . . . walk through

Note: Too many individuals play the "I wish" game instead of taking action. Dreams can never be achieved without taking those first steps and risking failure.

THE LIFE OF A PENCIL

It came out of the package shiny and yellow,
a pinkish eraser perched proudly on top,
a No. 2 lead imbedded within the hexagonal casing.
It was anxiously waiting to be sharpened
and placed in a hand so its use could commence.

In the beginning it stood straight and proud,
ready for any task that lay ahead,
excited for the journey upon which it would embark.
Meticulous care was taken at first,
chasing perfection was its desire,
limiting mistakes to conserve the eraser's life to match that of its own.
An occasional mark-through was used in its place,
designating a fork in the road.
Side notes were etched in the margin . . .
like little clues left to follow down a new, uncharted path.

Dizzying days were experienced as it was twirled in hand.
Music was interspersed when it was drummed on the desk—
both used to interject play in its youthful days.
Sometimes it was tapped on a chin while deep in thought,
mapping out the next steps to be taken.

But impetuosity set in as its days advanced.
Mistakes came more often as carelessness and impatience took root.
Its eraser diminished rapidly from the frustration of its errors.
Heavier mark-throughs began to appear with greater frequency,

displaying its growing edginess.
Neatness and order were gradually being discarded,
its days whittled down with more frequent sharpening.
The grinding noise—the symphony of diminishment.
The shavings—the evidence of its past, of lost time.
Could a return to the earlier days of attentive diligence slow its demise?
It was worth a try because there was still much left to do.

Its shortening stature was a reminder of its time dwindling away,
a reminder of its journey nearing its inevitable end.
Its life continued to be ground away until . . . one sharpening was left.
The work produced by its toil would be left behind as its testimonial,
of its time spent doing what was intended,
guided by the ever-present hand.

It is only fitting that its last act would be the period at the end of this
sentence,
its biography . . . now complete.

*Note: I had a pencil in my hand, jotting down ideas, so I thought, why not? You draw
your own conclusions or parallels from the poem.*

IN THE ZONE WITH THE RHYTHM AND BEAT

When I was a kid, it was a transistor radio,
with one earplug, playing rock-and-roll
over an AM band out of Dallas,
putting that rhythm and beat in my head,
a euphoric rush sweeping over me
as I road my bike down a hill to generate speed;
I thought it couldn't get much better than this.
I was in the zone.

In my teen years, the transistor radio was replaced
with the rumble and roar of my eight-track tape player,
pounding out the latest tunes as I rode in my car,
the windows rolled down . . . the wind in my hair,
cruising the streets of the small town in which I lived,
tapping my fingers on the steering wheel
to the rhythm and beat of the guitars and drums.
Speed was not a concern as the music played.
I was in no hurry . . . no destination in mind.
I was in a new and better zone.

Next came vinyl spinning on my turntable,
filling the room with the thump of the bass
and crystal-clear treble mixed in with the sound,
balanced with the midrange of the vocals in between,
unless . . . an offensive scratch caused a hiccup,
interrupting the flow of the rhythm and beat,
but the vinyl wasn't portable until copied to a cassette,

giving the music traveling legs,
allowing me to record and compile my favorites,
listening as I drove along . . . deep in the zone.

The little miniature version of an album came along
with the clarity of vinyl and portability of a cassette,
joined as one to create a CD (not a certificate of deposit),
coupled with a Walkman to play the disc.
The sweet rhythm and pulsating beat
could play anywhere or anytime;
add quality earphones to the mix
and an unbelievable sound was produced
to savor and possess for as long as the batteries held out.
I could now be in the zone 24/7.

It fit in my hand . . .
yet, was thinner than the old transistor radio I once possessed,
but the earbuds emitted a superior sound.
The amazing thing: it held hours of music and hundreds of songs,
downloaded and stored in the blink of an eye . . . well, maybe two.
I could strap it on my arm, taking it with me while out on a run,
the rhythm and beat taking my mind off any discomfort,
transporting me to a place of pleasure
while I sweated and toiled throughout the seasons,
keeping me in the zone all year long.

Playlists on a phone fill the bill with the current generation,
but I have experienced the full evolution.
The vinyl I have collected is back in style,
giving me a welcome trip down memory lane.
CD's I still have in ample supply,
and my little "Shuffle" still keeps me company on my runs.
I will even play a cassette every now and then.
The tunes, whether old or new, are still pleasant to hear.

They still make me tap my feet or sway with the sound;
I still pound on my thighs to an upbeat rock number.
For being in the zone with that rhythm and beat
never seems to get old . . . no matter my years.

Note: I heard someone mention transistor radio and it triggered my memories of listening to various types of music and the different devices upon which I listened. I have collected a variety of genres over the years on a variety of formats. Music has a special way of recalling events from our past, setting a mood, or just relaxing us in the moment.

LOOKING BACK TO LOOK AHEAD

I'm old enough to be a walking history lesson,
to have seen a lot of firsts—
    the first man in orbit,
    the first steps on the moon,
    the first heart transplant,
    the first joint replacement,
    the first Super Bowl,
    the first cordless phone,
    the first cellphone,
    the first Apple computer,
    the first hand-held (or pocket) calculator,
    the first CD player,
    the first video games,
    the first . . . you get the point.
But will anyone stop to ask of these firsts?
Or will they just press on,
showing no interest in what came before . . .
in what . . . or who laid the groundwork
for the current set of firsts in their current world.

Why is there little to no interest in bygone days?
Is nostalgia left to the old and weary?
Is it the age of the messenger or the message being delivered?
Is conversation between the generations . . . lost?
    the older . . . feeling ignored and irrelevant;
    the younger . . . focused on what comes next—
    their new set of firsts, not . . . what was.

Has the patience to stop and listen disappeared?

The telling of stories is a dying art.
It takes time for a good telling.
It is more than watching a YouTube.
It requires the teller to engage others with words,
which paint a picture for all to see,
capturing the imagination,
taking others to another place and time.
It requires the listener to focus on the telling—
    to pause and listen with calm diligence,
    to put aside the busyness of life for a while,
    to take in the story and allow it to come to life,
    to see the time spent in the telling and the listening as worthwhile.
For the story can build a bridge from the past,
telling where we have been
and pointing the way to where we would like to go,
linking the teller and the listener,
developing an appreciation and respect
for what was . . . and what could be.

Note: I remember sitting around with my dad and his friends when I was a young boy, listening to stories from the days of their youth. It seems we have lost that connection between the generations—a connection built upon the memories and stories of our past. Conversation is becoming a lost art. When it disappears, the bridge to our past will be gone, and with it, the stories which will help lead us into what lies ahead.

ARE YOU ALL IN?

I can't do it.
> Can't? or won't?
> Have you put forth the time and effort?
> Have you completely bought in with heart and soul?

I just can't do it. It's hard.
> Nothing easy is worthwhile, or everyone would do it.
> It takes commitment and perseverance.
> It takes single-minded focus and patience.

You just don't understand.
> Let me introduce you to Chris.
> He is twenty-one and has just completed his first Ironman—
>> 2.4 miles swimming,
>> 112 miles on a bike,
>> 26.2 miles running—
> all in less than 17 hours.
> He decided to change his life three years ago—
>> to work hard and train,
>> to become a better version of himself.
> It took him thirteen months, training six days a week.
> His three-step plan was not elaborate:
>> get 1% better each day;
>> work hard;
>> don't ever give up.
> Oh . . . I forgot to mention . . . Chris has Down's Syndrome.
> He wanted to do something that hadn't been done before.

He wanted to be the first—

 to inspire and pave the way for others,

 to be included in a world which we call "normal".

Shouldn't we aspire to be part of his world?

to be something special.

Whatever you are trying to accomplish, just follow his simple plan:

 get better little by little;

 just keep working;

 do not be discouraged and quit.

So, do you still think you can't?

I can at least try to get it done.

 That is always the first and most important step.

Note: Chris Nikic received the Jimmy V Award for perseverance at the 2021 ESPY's. His inspiring story demonstrates what can be accomplished when one is committed to improve a little every day. It just takes time, patience, and perseverance.

IT COULD HAPPEN

I watched a grown man achieve his boyhood dream.
At 71, he was able to fly to the edge of space,
becoming weightless for about four minutes.
It was the fulfillment of seventeen years of planning and building.
Upon landing, he displayed the thrill and joy of his youth,
jumping and smiling from ear to ear as he celebrated.
He recounted his youthful days,
building the spaceship of his boyhood days out of cardboard boxes,
dreaming of flying into space one day,
remembering those days as if it were yesterday.
I wonder what his parents thought of his dream.
Did they really believe? or just give him a smile of encouragement,
thinking this fad would pass.

It reminded me of my grandson at the age of four—
    that age when all things seem possible,
     when belief in the magic of his imagination is still very real.
Holland was going through a "space phase,"
and he really looked cute in his replica astronaut suit,
complete with matching helmet, which his Gigi had bought for him.
My part was to build him a rocket ship out of cardboard.
After a couple of hours of intense work, with Holland at my side—
    and the aid of scissors, tape, and staples—
the ship was completed and ready for launch.
We placed the ship in the backyard
because the ship obviously couldn't be launched from indoors—
    that would have been quite messy.

Holland's dad had placed sparklers around the cardboard craft,
simulating the rocket's blast.
The young astronaut marched out of the house all decked out in his suit
to the resounding cheer of us all as we watched him step into the ship.
Holland buckled himself into the seat, and the countdown commenced.
We began to shake the rocket as it readied for takeoff,
a great roar sounding as the rocket blasted off.
In his mind, my grandson was flying into outer space,
making its maiden voyage to the sun.
The ship of cardboard had become the real thing.
His dream was being realized.

As I continued to watch the interview, I couldn't help but think . . .
maybe Holland will make it to space one day.
The man was saying he hoped to be flying people to space in a year or
two—
       the price tag: $250,000.
If Holland and I start saving our allowance . . .
It could happen.
Isn't that why we dream?

Note: Sir Richard Branson achieved his dream, making what seemed improbable, very much a possibility. It is quite possible my grandson will achieve his dream one day. Maybe his Papa can make the trip with him. One can dream.

PERSPECTIVE

It must happen now.
Waiting is inconvenient.
Time is of the essence.
Be bold and act.
Impetuosity is not the word applied.
To wait is to be tentative.
Until . . . mistakes due to rashness occur.
Hindsight now deems the waiting as patience.
Now . . . regret sets in.

It can wait—maybe another day will do.
The time isn't right.
Other things are more pressing.
To wait now gives procrastination a positive slant.
Patience is now plentiful with justification's rationale.
Until . . . the waiting is no longer needed.
The waiting is taken away by life's unexpected turns.
Opportunities have been snatched away.
Now . . . regret sets in.

Note: To wait or not to wait. It's a matter of perspective. Human nature is to put the twist of justification on any decision which tends to go awry. We don't won't to own our mistakes.

JUST A CONVERSATION AWAY

Their pursuit is relentless . . . untiring.
They will never show mercy,
determined to taint emotions
with disgrace . . . with embarrassment.

The attempt to run and hide,
to seek refuge and shelter,
is becoming a doomed objective;
to outrun them is not possible.

Realization is setting in.
Escape is unattainable,
the inevitable surrender, forthcoming
to the twin tormentors—shame and guilt.

They will leave reminders.
Some mementos are self-inflicted.
Some are constant rebukes
from a ruthless audience.

So . . .
How can the anguish be quelled?
How can the remorse be banished?
How can the mental torture be exiled?
How can the self-reproach be expelled?

Forgiveness is the only antidote,

sincerely sought . . . earnestly desired,

a heartfelt yearning to be pardoned,

yet willing to deal with the consequences.

Humanity sometimes pardons and forgets.

Oftentimes, its memory is long and unwavering,

but divine forgiveness is always offered.

It's just a quiet conversation away.

Note: We often forget that God is ready and willing to forgive even though we are reluctant to forgive ourselves or others who have wronged us. Only He knows the sincerity that lies within the heart of those asking for forgiveness.

LIFE'S WINTER SEASON

The days of autumn have disappeared.
Winter is fast approaching,
    bitter arctic blasts sweeping in,
    the cold reaching into the bone's marrow,
    its spirit-depressing bitterness, unwelcome and unwanted.
The days of spring have long since evaporated—
    vague memories of a forgone season,
    days longed for as the final season sets in.
The more winter advances, the greater the desire to retreat
    to those lost days of spring.
The end is closing in, as it must, its inevitability preordained.
Life's cycle must be completed.
Be thankful the cycle wasn't cut short in an earlier season,
    for a life reaching winter has been full.
Its reward—the memories of past seasons.
What lies beyond life's season of winter?
Isn't that a journey worth anticipating?

Note: I was sitting and reflecting on my life and pondering what comes next.

REFUSE TO BE BEAT

He played all year with a knee in need of repair
    but won a Super Bowl.
He defeated cancer on his way back to the ice,
    becoming one of the NHL's all-time best.
She overcame knee surgery to win the Olympic Marathon.

These are the notable, the ones who catch our eye,
but countless others, unknown to us, fight battles every day,
in all walks of life, from every corner of our world.
They are young and old, child and adult, male and female.
Their struggle to survive tragedy, to overcome injury, to conquer disease,
to face the eventuality of death when all efforts have failed
illustrates the human spirit at its best.

The stories of the human spirit's refusal
to give in against insurmountable odds, its indomitable resolve,
its willingness to sacrifice so others can carry on the fight
have inspired us when we seemed ready to be counted out.
They give us the needed boost to renew our own personal grapples
when life is attempting to knock us out of the game.
Our own spirit can once again soar with eagles on high,
run with the swiftest of antelopes,
roar with the mightiest of lions.
It is in these moments we experience the fullness of all life offers,
believing once again in what is possible.

The human spirit can't be beat if it refuses to be beat.

It carries on even after death has defeated its physical vessel.

It is fueled by memories of triumphs from past ages.

It is fueled by the anticipation of fantastic triumphs yet to come.

As long as the memories last and the stories are told,

the spirit will live on in the hearts . . .

and minds of those who refuse to be beat.

Note: I was watching a story on the national news how a young man worked his way back from cancer in his leg to rejoin and play with his high school basketball team. The story documented his unwavering resolve to make it back. His story is a reminder of how much the human spirit can help us to overcome whatever obstacles are placed in our path.

THE LONG ROAD BACK

Upon leaving the hospital with a new titanium hip,
the realization of advancing age hit home,
weighing on my mind with uncertainties to be answered—
    would I be able to leap tall buildings (maybe this was a dream)?
    what will be the new normal?
    how much strength and flexibility could I regain?
    what about my balance and stability?
    will my patience be adequate?
The long road I must travel is indeterminate in length;
the journey down this road may never end,
one whose path might be filled with detours and side-trips.
Only time will answer the questions milling around in my mind.

But to have a sense of youthful invincibility once again—
the feeling that life and all its possibilities stretch out beyond the horizon
of time;
the belief that the race against Father Time can be won;
to experience the exhilaration of chasing untapped potential—
is a yearning pulling hard on my spirit,
a tricky balancing act between what was and what might be.
The "what was" keeps me hoping for what could be again.
The "what might be" could be frustrating if expectations are foolhardy.

Perseverance . . . persistence . . . determination . . . resolve . . .
All have been learned and honed with the experience of years.
All will be companions upon which to lean heavily during this journey,
companions with whom I will travel on this long road back.

Note: I had hip replacement surgery in June of 2021. The pain relief was immediate, but the uncertainty about how close to normal my activities could become weighed on me. I can only take it one day at a time, one step at a time, determined to do all that could be done, while understanding my quality of life would be much improved post-surgery as compared to pre-surgery.

MONUMENT

The old cemetery needed mowing.
Many of the old monuments were in disrepair.
Some had even toppled over—
    others on the verge, like some miniature version of the leaning tower.
Names were hidden by mold, engravings almost completely faded away.
Who were they?
I couldn't help but wonder what kind of life they had lived.
Was there anyone left who could recall their walk on this Earth?
Or was their time just forgotten—
    never to be remembered,
    their presence long since erased,
    a broken piece of stone the only mark left of their life.

I realized I didn't want a hunk of granite to mark my span of time,
a monument to be ignored after two or three generations.
I don't want others to cry for me when my earthly time comes to an end,
for my life has been full of purpose and meaning.
I want a walking, talking, breathing, living monument to mark my time—
    one that can pass on shared stories of our time together;
    one that can pass on lessons learned working side by side;
    one that can share their life with the ones they love,
    planting their own seeds
    for the next generation . . . and the next . . . and the next.

I don't want anyone to look for me at the foot of a slab of stone.
I want others to look for the fruit of my labor in the generations I have left behind,
for they are my memorial . . . my living monument.

Note: The age of sixty is in my rearview mirror which makes me reflect even more on my life, contemplating what will be my monument to the time I was granted. Will others view my time as well spent? or wasted?

UNTIL

I felt blessed until someone told me I had been deprived
I never knew what I was missing until I saw what I didn't have

I never felt unwanted until no one chose me
I never felt unloved until others criticized me

I never felt cheated until someone took from me
I was trusting until I found I had been lied to

I was content until someone pointed out I should desire more
I was happy until someone questioned my happiness

I was an optimist until someone told me it wasn't practical
I was a dreamer until someone told me it wasn't possible

Later . . .

I was lost and alone until I was found
I was an outcast until others took me in

I was hopeless until others offered to help
I felt scorned until others accepted me

I was groping blindly until someone took my hand
I felt adrift until someone cast me a lifeline

I felt guilt and regret until someone forgave me

I felt shame until I was shown the path of repentance

I felt broken until someone helped me fix my brokenness
My life was in pieces until others helped me put the pieces in place

Note: People are so easily torn down by the words and actions of others. It takes the care and help of others to lead the broken back to a life of meaning and purpose, acceptance and love.

FINDING MY WAY

Staggering around, lost with a sense of foreboding.
Darkness is closing around me, engulfing my troubled mind;
I need to find my way back.
I look to the darkening sky with a prayerful attitude—

hoping to find some answer to my dilemma,

searching for some cosmic sign to aid me—
when I notice the North Star glowing brighter than all the other stars in
God's heaven,

drawing my eye to its brilliance as it hangs suspended in its celestial
realm.
It is the signpost for which I have been searching—

the signpost upon which I can fix my bearing,

using it to determine north from south and east from west.
My breathing slows . . . my spirit calms . . .
This heavenly compass will guide me on my way.

Note: When one is lost, it's as simple as looking heavenward to find the way back.

WORK IN PROGRESS

To invite trials is to invite growth.
To invite trials is to invite pain and suffering—
 no pain . . . no gain.
To invite, means to choose—
 to understand what is required,
 to understand what is needed to improve,
 to understand the journey of sacrifice
 leads to a desirable reward at the end.
Diligence and patience over time are essential;
otherwise, the journey will be abandoned.
Once again, a choice is involved—
 quit . . . or carry on.

What about uninvited trials?
What about uninvited pain and suffering?
A choice is still given—
 whine and complain . . . or endure through faith.
Isn't this an invitation to grow?
Isn't this an invitation to flex spiritual muscle?
 to understand testing is part of growing,
 to understand I am still a work in progress in His hands,
 to be improved and perfected through trial,
 to demonstrate determined perseverance,
 to understand this journey of sacrifice
 leads to the ultimate reward at journey's end.
Then His work in me will be complete.

Note: Choice is about control. We can choose to exercise, eat properly, learn new things. It is our choice, and we invite the struggles that come with those choices. Why can't we accept the struggles which are not part of our choosing? When we accept with faith these unwanted trials, we can become stronger through our dependence on God, understanding He will help and guide us through all our struggles.

DIFFICULT LESSONS

The well-being of our children is paramount—
>hours upon hours of worrying and fretting;
>plans formulated and reformulated;
>every precaution taken—
>attempting to keep them safe from harm,
>attempting to keep them from the ravages of self-doubt,
>attempting to build and grow self-esteem—
>wanting the best for their present and future.

But somehow, it has been forgotten that
>allowing them to stumble and fall
>>gives them the opportunity to pick themselves up,
>>allowing them to fail
>>gives them the opportunity to learn failure is okay as long as they don't quit,
>>allowing them to make mistakes
>>gives them the chance to correct and learn.

These are the most difficult lessons a parent can experience
because it involves dealing with
>their own pain . . .
>their own self-doubt . . .
>their own sense of failure . . .

leaving them to wonder if they are doing it right.
Only time can give them any sense of comfort.
Only time can lay to rest this uncertainty.
For now, just keep loving . . . keep nurturing . . . keep learning.

Note: My kids are all grown and out on their own. These lessons were the most difficult to learn but the most helpful for their well-being.

WERE YOU LISTENING?

Are you listening?

I hear you.

That's not what I asked.

I heard what you said.

But did you understand what I said?

Did you put your phone aside and look at me?

Did you focus on my words and their meaning?

Did they have any impact on your thoughts?

or were they just some extraneous noise

to be discarded as unimportant.

So, were you listening to what I said?

Well . . . maybe I wasn't.

Note: I was watching two people looking at their phones and attempting to carry on a conversation with each other. I was wondering how much understanding was going on between them. My dad was always big on looking at the person who was talking to you.

SCHOOL STARTING 2021

Summer is coming to a close.
Another school year is about to begin,
another year full of excitement and expectation.
Vaccinations are allowing us to unmask if we choose.
Maybe we are going to beat this virus yet.

The new variant is beginning to surge;
Delta has its own set of plans.
It is fighting for its survival just as nature intends,
refusing to go down without a fight.
It is searching for new victims upon which it can attack.

Politicians are going back and forth on whether to mandate masks once
again.
Some shout individual choice should be the policy,
but can those be trusted with the safety of others?
while others want to require masks until this new variant subsides.
It is a perfect backdrop for this political theater.

Some schools are beginning with mask requirements.
Personal choice has been taken out of the equation for now.
The welfare and safety of all is considered paramount.
Protesters are still pushing back against this edict,
while others are applauding, hoping this keeps their children safe.

I see students walking the halls with masks in place.
I reflect back on the school opening of 2020,
and it looks eerily similar.

The difference: students are in person on Day 1,
not camped in front of a screen.

Is this progress?
It looks like baby steps,
but . . .
we can still hope;
we can still pray.

Note: Teachers came back after the summer without having to wear a mask. We all thought the worst was behind us, that normalcy was returning. Two days before we were to welcome our students back, masks were required to be worn once again. Two steps forward, one step back.

WHAT IT MEANS TO TEACH

Look beneath what you see,
past the façade of fake bravado
or the mask of self-doubt.

Find the spirit buried beneath the shell,
a spirit crying out to be rescued,
desiring to see the dawn of a new day.

Envision what they could be,
then help them become that vision—
what they never thought they could be.

Help them to dream about what is possible,
then show them how to achieve all that is possible . . .
maybe even what is . . . impossible.

Demonstrate care and concern for them
when they are swallowed up with despair,
when they feel no one seems to care.

Be there when they stumble and fall,
offering an encouraging hand so they can rise.
Be that support upon which they can trust.

For some, simply guide their curiosity,
helping them to explore and discover,
training them that failure is just another path to learning.

For some, the lamp of learning is burning low;
to rekindle the light, so it burns bright, is the task,
helping them reclaim the joy which was once theirs.

Ultimately, send them on their life's journey—
self-assured, confident, full of hope, eager . . .
Impossible, many might say . . .

But this is what it means to teach.

Note: I have been a teacher for over forty years. This is what I and others like me have been trying to accomplish with students each year. It is an elusive quest but one which I continue to chase.

KINDERGARTNER'S FIRST DAY

I am looking at my grandson's picture on his first day of kindergarten.
His journey down his school path has officially begun,
scheduled to last at least thirteen years
unless he decides to extend his journey to a higher level.
He is dressed in his new uniform—navy polo and khaki shorts—
the smile on his face lighting up his eyes.
He has no way of knowing what the year has in store for him,
his young mind only processing one day at a time.
He will begin his work with the three Rs.
He will learn to cooperate and have a sense of fair play.
He will participate in school programs for his mom, dad, and little sis to
see.
His work will proudly adorn the refrigerator.
His mom and dad will guide and encourage his efforts,
helping him foster a love for school and learning,
relating the stories of their own school days.

Thus, begins the journey he and his parents will take together,
for it is a path which must be shared,
memories to be made and filed away,
to be reflected upon at a later date and time,
to maybe share with his own child one day.
Holland's first day report: It was awesome!

Note: The poem pretty much explains itself. I hope Holland's school journey is filled with joy and wonder, that this first year will just be the beginning of a marvelous journey.

ADOLESCENCE

stuck between two worlds
not a child; not an adult
just laboring in between

fighting the urges of childhood
wanting to test the adult arena
but not accepted in either

bodies awkwardly changing
girls advancing all too quickly
boys desperately playing catch-up

all actors playing their parts
rolls changing, in flux, transitioning
the interplay—a comedy of errors

a painful training ground of confusion
searching for avenues of expression
searching for ways to fit in

working to figure it all out
trial and error—the primary method
a profusion of mixed results

anxiety and stress—constant companions
frustration—unwilling to accept mistakes
impatience—immediate gratification is required

ready to pledge undying love
but not really understanding what love is
at least, not the sacrificial part

pliable, moldable, a fillable vessel
in the right hands, a work of art
the challenge—finding the right hands

Note: I watch students struggle with adjusting during their initial years in high school. It is a painful thing to watch at times, this trying to adjust and fit in. When they can find the right mentors and friends, the possibilities open up, and their world becomes a welcome place in which they can explore and develop.

SENIOR YEAR

They come through the doors, excitement evident in their eyes,
joy in their voice, a spring in their step.
Their laughter is echoing in the halls on this first day,
expectations soaring, eagerly anticipating this most special of years.
The finish line is near but not yet crossed.

The first days of their school journey are vague now,
only snippets of memory remain,
but pictures of miniature versions of themselves can be retrieved,
replete with smiles on that very first day,
backpack in hand with the essential supplies,
ready for the initial step down this path called school,
not knowing what this journey would bring,
just seeing the joy on a parent's face, with a tear or two mixed in.

Now . . . they face the year with eyes looking forward,
surveying the possibilities of what lies ahead.
Some have had an easier journey, some more difficult,
but they are all at the doorstep no matter what path was taken.
They are anxious for the events awaiting them—
the contests, games, dances, concerts, performances . . .
but not necessarily the classes and projects—
all designed to test their academic acumen—
for they will be challenged on the field, on the court, in the classroom.
But isn't that what growth is all about?
to be tested, to become better, to strive for a dream,
to experience triumph and the euphoria with which it is entwined—

all the while remaining humble, for defeat is always lurking close by;
to overcome failure, for this is where the true lessons are learned
because the failing doesn't matter—
it's the willingness to try again that is the true measure of a person.

They will be building memories during this final year
which will last through their journey beyond these halls,
memories which will forever unite them—
    classmates bonded together, walking arm in arm down memory lane.
Stories of exploits will be told again and again—
    the retelling allowing them to become a little grander over time—
friendships deepening . . . being enriched from the sharing.

But this special year will also be about the aid rendered
when the load seems overwhelming—
    a shoulder to lean on;
    a sympathetic ear, ready to listen;
    a reassuring embrace;
    an encouraging pat on the back;
    or a swift kick if it's needed.
Friendships will grow from these trials,
strengthened by the struggling together,
learning they are not alone and should not be alone,
that asking for help is not a sign of weakness
but a realization that together they are stronger.

This is a year to embrace each day for what it can be,
to relish the opportunities awaiting,
to master the fear of failure and keep trying,
to understand this year is meant to be special—
    a rite of passage onto a bigger stage for which they are preparing—
to look back and not be filled with regrets,
to run and not crawl across the finish line,
for there is only one senior year.

Note: I was watching students come in the doors on the first day and was reminded of past seniors who began their final year filled with anticipation, watching them grow together throughout the course of the year.

GRADUATION DAY

On this your graduation day,
pause . . . reflect . . . remember
> those who have loved and nurtured you through these years,
> those who have provided structure and discipline so you could understand boundaries,
> those who have encouraged you through your trials and struggles,
> those who have always had your back when detractors came at you from all sides.

Remember the diploma you will soon hold in your hand is not the end of your learning;
it is the beginning.
For instruction will continue from your most demanding instructor—life.
The lessons you must learn along the next phase of your journey
> will determine success . . . or failure.
Don't fear the challenges you meet;
they will help you grow as you travel along life's twisting and winding road.
For learning occurs
> when you are removed from your comfort zone,
> when you are forced to test your abilities,
> when you suffer setbacks (they are not failures unless you quit the game),
> when you search for solutions which seem beyond your reach.

Remember you were not meant to make this journey alone.
Seek out those who can aid you as you navigate this path.
Surround yourself with mentors who will bring out your best;
you are the only one who will or can limit . . . you.

Develop true friendships where you both hold each other accountable in every way,

forging lifelong bonds which will withstand the onslaught

of all the naysayers and doubters trying to deter you as you march along.

Remember to be a source of encouragement springing from the wellspring of hope.

Be part of the solution for a better day for all of humanity.

It is better to jump into the fray instead of passively watching from the side,

for true courage occurs when you are willing to ride into the teeth of the battle

even though you are filled with fear and apprehension.

Remember

love and kindness,

respect and courtesy,

compassion and empathy . . . will never go out of style.

Remember to squeeze every ounce of joy out of each day you are given,

for it is a blessing from God to be used for His good purposes.

So, enjoy your Earthly journey with every fiber in your soul

until you reach the final bend in your road and . . .

He reaches out His hand on your final graduation day.

Note: I wrote this at the close of the COVID school year as a message of hope for our graduating seniors. My wish is that they will go out and approach their future with hope and joy.

FIND THAT SOMETHING

What brings happiness to the life we live?
a question that has been examined from every angle.
It has been dissected and analyzed . . . inspected and scrutinized.
Its secret has been sought throughout the ages—
linked with wealth, fame, success, satisfaction . . .

Consider this for a beginning:
Look deep inside and find your passion—
    something that brings you joy,
    something that makes you laugh,
    something that makes you jump out of bed,
    something that gives your day purpose,
    something that lights up your soul for all to see,
    something that inspires you to be the best version of you,
    something that fills you with hope,
    something that helps you see the wonders of His creation.
Then you will never work a day in your life,
For it's never work if you're doing what you love.

Note: The 2020–21 school year is ending, and I hear students making their plans for their future careers. So many base their plans on a paycheck. I give the advice contained in this poem to students every year.

FATHER'S DAY

This is a day to honor and remember the life that you lived,
a life not perfect . . . but still honored and cherished.

This is the first without your physical presence
but the honoring and remembering still go on.
I am not sad.
I don't feel cheated at your passing.

I would still like to have you here to honor,
but I know this is part of life.

So, I will carry on remembering,
with a smile and an occasional laugh,
all that you meant to me
and the others who miss your humor and wit.

On this day and every day,
I will choose to honor your life.

Note: The poem pretty much states where my mind was on Father's Day 2021. I still remember my dad with a smile on my face. He lived a full life helping others.

TRADITION

The old man was sitting on his porch,
rocking away the morning,
anticipating the gathering of the clan,
thinking of the past times
when all had assembled to celebrate,
a time steeped in ceremony,
layered with years of reminiscences.

The whole event was repetitive in nature,
adhering to a prescribed schedule—
eating the same foods;
expectations of predictable activities;
a shared conviction that all must be fulfilled;
that the fulfillment is in the best interests of many,
building mutual memories to pass on.

To vary the routine, accentuates a feeling of unease,
enhancing a collective desire for a return
to what is comfortable . . . to what is customary,
strengthening the need to remain devoted
to the beginnings through which all are connected,
a common thread weaving throughout the generations,
linking the stories to be told and retold.

The old man began to smile as the cars arrived,
descending on the homeplace as if on cue.
Taking a break from his rocking,

he hollered inside, "They're here."
He greeted those arriving with hugs—
the missus bursting through the door
with shouts of joy, joining in the welcome.

The air filled with the sounds of laughter
as everyone began to walk indoors,
the familiar smells from the past
adding their own welcome to the festivities,
anticipation of the good times to be experienced
filling the home with warmth and enthusiasm,
reinforcing the cherished bonds of family.

Note: Tradition links the generations, providing a way to connect and reconnect, building the memories which are necessary to create lasting bonds of familial love.

WHEN ALL IS STRIPPED AWAY

What happens when the veneer is gone?
What is left when all pretense is stripped away?
What is the essence of what is left?

Is it insecure and jaded?
 beat down by adversity;
 discouraged because of failure;
 full of pessimism because of persecution;
 arrogance masking self-doubt.

Or is it pure and trusting?
 built on faith in something greater;
 radiant with hope, regardless of circumstances;
 full of love and selflessness;
 full of peace from sacred promises.

So . . . which is it?
What is left exposed for others to see?
 one turning inward with self-pity and resentment,
 searching for pleasure and satisfaction in what can be gained;
 or one emanating from inner strength, impervious to assailants,
 searching for ways to give and bring pleasure and joy to others.

Because in the end . . .
all will be stripped away;
all that will be left is the soul to judge.
All the trappings of this life . . . must be left behind.

Note: I heard somewhere the question: What is left when everything has been stripped away? I started thinking about the emotional state of people and what they deem important and coupled this question with the expression: You can't take it with you. It is a poem of self-examination for anyone who might read the words.

A MESSAGE FROM GOD

Your little girl is peacefully sleeping—
such a big fighter in so small a package.
She is in my protective hands
    where I can give strength and provide comfort.
Mom, I know you are living a parent's worst nightmare,
but come to Me for strength . . . for comfort . . . for peace.
Place yourself in My protective hands,
for this is where all My children belong.
Your little one is special to Me, as are you, so
    unburden yourself,
    calm yourself,
    love yourself.
Remember, I am always just a whisper away.

Note: A teaching colleague reached out to our staff for prayers and words of encouragement for a friend whose little girl was in critical condition. This poem was sent to her in hopes it would offer peace and comfort during this time. Her little girl pulled through and is doing well.

GIVE BACK

We are called to
    clean the unclean,
    help the helpless,
    encourage the discouraged,
    love the unlovable,
    forgive the unforgivable.

While understanding, we are to
    give without receiving,
    serve without being served,
    contribute with no expectation,
    help without acclaim,
    love when it is not returned.

Why?
    Because it was done for us.

Note: I was thinking about what needs to happen if humanity is to vanquish the ills which plague our world.

STEP BY STEP

Tired . . . so tired . . . totally spent.
I can't take another step.
The long road ahead goes on and on and on,
disappearing into the distant horizon.

Ready to give up.
Ready to cash in my chips.
Ready for it all to end.
 Take a deep breath.
Who is that?
 Take a deep breath and let it out.
 Calm yourself.
I look around but don't see anyone.
 Clear you mind of the clutter.
 Focus on My voice.
I sense a presence.
The voice is calm and reassuring.
A glimmer of hope surfaces.
 Take one step . . . then take another.
But I insist, I can't.
 Trust me.
 You can.
I begin with one step . . . then another.
 I will be with you step after step.
 Just keep putting one foot in front of the other.
Despair was fleeing; hope was growing.
I refocused on the road directly in front of me,

knowing the journey would still be difficult,

but I no longer felt isolated and alone.

I have now been joined by a new companion.

Note: We are all tired of life in the pandemic. Call out for help during this time of unrest, knowing that God is always ready to join in the journey.

COMPLETE SURRENDER

sliding down a slippery slope
looking for a way to put on the brakes
suffering from my own faulty decisions
I finally stopped my mental chastising
and remembered these words:

> Trust in the Lord with all your heart
>> *fully, completely, unwavering, with no reservations*
>
> and lean not on your own understanding;
>> *throw out what you know or what you think you know*
>> *don't depend on anyone else's knowledge*
>> *lean on God and His knowledge of your heart and mind*
>
> in all your ways submit to Him,
>> *yield to His authority; defer to His judgement*
>> *remove yourself from the equation; surrender to His will*
>
> and He will make your paths straight.
>> *you will never be lost again*
>> *you will never wander needlessly*
>> *he will guide you on your journey the rest of your days*

But if free will and choice should make me stumble,
for they will
should my human judgement lead me astray,
and it will
I must return to the beginning with humble contrition and start anew.
He is patient and will forgive
His greatest joy is for me to have faith and trust.

for out of this I can eternally live

Note: We fail often in our relationships with others. We lose focus and get lost on our life journey. Proverbs 3: 5–6 is the best and most difficult advice by which we can model our life. God is more than willing to forgive when we stray from the path He has intended for us.

WHY DO I DO WHAT I DO?

Thoughtful actions, kind words, helpful efforts . . .
Isn't life about the care of others, serving others?
So, why feel disheartened when no one recognizes the effort?
Is the recognition needed?
Are these deposits in some type of emotional bank necessary?
Is the withdrawal at some future date to be used to pat myself on the back?
Why am I doing what I do?

    to gain favor?

    to earn love?

    to earn acceptance?

    to work my way to a heavenly realm?

Are my words an empty gesture lacking sincerity?
Am I trying to gain leverage by reminding others of my efforts?

Maybe I need to examine my motivation.

    Do I really have a servant's heart?

    Does my attitude align with what God intended?

    Does my life reflect selfless devotion?

    Do I receive true joy from uplifting others? watching them grow and prosper.

If not . . .
It is time for some quiet time in divine conversation.

Note: Always be careful of the motivation behind what we do. We will never be good enough to earn our way to heaven's door. We serve out of gratitude for God's gift to us.

THE RETURNING

I lift my eyes heavenward, searching for you.
I remember reading you are always present and watching,
available to all who would reach out, a benevolent God.
Why has pain and sorrow camped at my doorstep?
I have prayed for the healing of my loved one.
I have reached out, but you don't seem to be listening.
Are you there?
Do you hear me?
I will do whatever you want if you will just grant my prayer.
You can take whatever you want from me.

I buried my face in my hands—
dejected and despondent . . . discouraged and downhearted.
What is left to do?
I am consumed with this feeling of isolation;
I feel stranded with no help in sight.

A message seems to be assembling in my mind.
Thoughts begin to flash in and out like a bad signal trying to tune in,
staticky at first . . . but slowly becoming clearer.
The message shakes me to my core.

Why do you only seek Me when misfortune strikes?
Why do you seldom reach out to Me during your daily journey?
just to talk . . . to acknowledge My presence in your life.
I want you to be open with Me even though I know your every thought,
sharing your dreams, giving thanks for the blessings you have been granted—

food, a home, a job, family, your capacity to love.
I have provided a way for you to receive all of these.
My subtle presence has guided you because of My love for you.
I know your heart.
I know you are troubled.
I know the desperation which is burying you.
I know you are treating Me as an afterthought . . . as a last resort.
Do you think I am here only for your convenience?
to answer your cry and rescue you from your misfortunes.
I don't want you to bargain out of selfish need.
I can do all things with or without you.
It is for your benefit when you help and serve Me.
I am watching over your loved one.
They are not alone in their struggle.
Draw comfort from this promise.
Have peace in your soul knowing I am in control
even if that might mean calling your loved one to be with Me,
to come to their eternal home full of peace and joy
where they will never know sorrow or heartache,
where they will never know pain or discomfort.
I leave you now to think on these words;
then offer up your prayers to Me with a selfless attitude,
remembering My unconditional love for you.
It will never waver . . . even when you tend to forget Me.

These thoughts were too clear to be my imagination.
The insights hit the mark dead-center,
but they didn't leave me in anguish or with a beaten down spirit.
Instead of being filled with grief and guilt, I felt hope.
I was filled with an unexpected calm . . . an unanticipated peace.
I never sensed the message to be one of righteous retribution
but more of an invitation to return home as after a long absence.
I bowed my head in reverence and felt a sense of welcome.
I began to speak and get reacquainted.

Note: This poem hits close to home. I go through periods where I get caught up in the busyness of my life and forget all my blessings. The tragic events which I see on television, the homeless I observe on the streets, the death of family and friends gives me pause to refocus my priorities and give thanks for the life I have been granted and the time I have been given to serve.

LIFE'S PURPOSE

Live life with reckless abandon—
>no safety net,
>no fall back.

Full speed ahead—
>no tapping on the brakes,
>no slowing down in the curves.

Throw caution to the wind—
>no deliberation,
>no speculation necessary.

Leave others in my wake—
>no looking behind,
>no quarter asked or given.

If this be my creed, then . . .

Reckless abandon has consequences—
>no regard for what might happen,
>no concern of any harm done.

Full speed leaves no margin for error—
>no distress over mistakes made,
>no consideration for errors in judgment.

Ignoring caution is to disregard warnings—
>no thought given to forewarning,
>no recognition of cues for failure.

Leaving others behind is isolating—
>no comradery,
>no shared experiences.

What about considering slight tweaks, such as . . .

Live life with reckless abandon in the pursuit of what is right and good
when facing those who are in opposition.

Warnings are ignored when given by those
who would stand in the way of goodness and mercy.

To carry on the fight for what is deemed virtuous and honorable
is not a task which many will follow or desire to follow—
the fear of retribution causing the faint of spirit to fall to the side.

But I know I will never fight alone.
A heavenly presence will always be by my side,
encouraging me, guiding me to do what is right and good,
providing the safety net that is needed.

For life or death is not the consideration,
only what is right in the face of what is wrong.

*Note: I heard the phrase, live life with reckless abandon, and thought of the parameters
under which this might be done. This poem is a reflection on the dangers of this attitude
but also the boldness when it is appropriately applied.*

HUMBLY GIVEN

It was given quietly . . . humbly,
without pomp or show.

The amount given wouldn't have bought very much,
but it was given sacrificially out of love.

It was all she had to give,
but no hesitation did she display.

The gift was accepted with a smile
and recorded as an example for others to follow.

No gift is meaningless.
No gift is too small.

For it wasn't the size or worth that mattered
but the sincerity with which it was given.

Note: What is the motive behind giving? Are there strings attached, something expected in return? I was reading about the elderly woman who gave all she had and wrote this short and simple poem. Any gift, when given sincerely, is always welcome because the receiver can sense the care and love with which it was given. Never hesitate to give even when the size of the gift seems too small.

THE MAGIC OF BELIEVING

Where has the magic of believing gone?
a belief in the goodness of others.
Is it lost forever down some rabbit hole?
or are we just sidetracked, misguided by doubt,
now groping blindly to rediscover a path back.

When does the magic of believing disappear?
replaced by a wearied and troubled demeanor,
no longer looking at life with enthusiastic anticipation,
only anticipating pain . . . sorrow . . . dejection . . .
hope fading . . . peace of mind perishing—
    suspicion replacing trust;
    despair replacing joy;
    pessimism replacing optimism;
    skepticism replacing faith;
    apathy replacing caring.

Can we ever view the world once again
with wide-eyed wonder and joy,
such as a child at Christmas,
awaiting the arrival of their wished-for gifts,
firmly believing in the existence of that "jolly old elf";

or trust with the unwavering conviction of our youth,
when it was thought that flight was possible
after reading comics or watching some movie with heroes in flight;
all that was needed was to tie on a cape, take a running start,

and allow our imagination to take control;

or delight in the uncharted waters of new experiences,
like that of innocent love when holding hands is a thrill,
our hearts pounding in anticipation of the first kiss,
and when it happens . . . our spirit takes flight . . . it soars,
leaving us desperate for one more before saying goodnight;

or revel in the euphoria of new beginnings,
like starting a journey with that special person,
each one committed to love unfailingly,
each one committed to support unceasingly,
two hearts . . . two lives . . . entwined and in sync;

or bask in the glow of unbridled elation,
like that which blooms with a baby's birth
and keeps growing with that baby's first steps,
many more moments to be added to the memory book
so the elation can be recalled when it seems to fade.

More and more, when looking across the landscape of humanity,
selfish ambition is leading to anger when that ambition is unfulfilled,
leading to discord—bordering on hatred—
the finger of blame leading to more dissension,
isolating us . . . denying us the fellowship of others.

So how can a bridge be built from suspicion back to trust?
where once again the belief in goodness can flourish.
Could it be that faith must be plugged into the equation?
a faith in an unseen guide pointing to the gateway back,
leading to love, joy, hope, peace, kindness, selflessness—
all in harmonious accord, shaping a generous and caring spirit,
one experiencing the magic of believing once again.

Note: I started thinking about the phrase, the magic of believing, and began to associate it with our youth, when life is still full of eager anticipation before we are weighed down with responsibilities and disappointments. We tend to lose sight of what faith in God can give us in our daily lives, how that faith can give us the necessary support we need to regain the joy in living.

GIVING UP CONTROL

The face of worry has no age limits.
It can surface anywhere . . . anyplace . . . anytime—
the fidgeting, the hand wringing, the outbursts of anger,
the mental exhaustion, the fits of nervous energy;
all the outgrowth of
    the need to meet desires,
    the need to control outcomes,
    the need to exert will on others,
    the need for perfection;
unwilling to trust the end results to others
because only one path to the end is seen.

The continual mental anguish is now in control,
a dogged companion—every minute of every day—
removing any chance of serenity,
banishing any hope of relief;
just pestering questions of doubt—
    eroding assurances . . .
    undermining faith . . .
    feeding obsessions . . .

To pursue control is a fool's game;
to think control can be obtained is absurd;
to fret that control is lacking is a misuse of time.

But . . .
to understand . . . outside forces are beyond our control;

to understand . . . the way we react *is* in our control;
to understand . . . He *is* in control.
His result may not be what we want but . . . what we need.

This understanding is the beginning of faith.
This acceptance is to remove worry . . . to ease fears,
ushering in calm reassurance . . . genuine belief.

Note: I see the face of worry on small children, students, and adults. The need for control is an all-consuming desire being pursued by many individuals. It is an energy-sapping activity, leading to frustration's doorstep.

WHAT'S IT WORTH?

A lifetime spent chasing but never quite catching;
what will it take to have
    peace of mind,
    unceasing joy,
    unconditional love,
    undying hope,
    unbroken promises,
    total contentment.

What is the price tag attached?
Is the price too much to pay?
Would it be worth all that is owned?

To chase any with financial resources is to miss the point.
Any or all is priceless, but . . .
it all can be attained if the commitment is sincere.
No money down . . . no payment required—
    the sacrifice of time,
    the sacrifice of self,
    the sacrifice of pride,
    the sacrifice of vain ambition.
All are deemed by the faithless as too steep a price.

The wanting is confused with what is needed.
This hunger for more causes blessings to be ignored.
This coveting causes those blessings to be underappreciated.
When is enough . . . enough?

Impatient . . . despondent . . . miserable with more.
Or satisfied . . . grateful . . . fulfilled with less.

For many, the chase will continue, the longing will magnify,
even when the solution is available and waiting;
for those it's like crawling through the eye of a needle;
for others, it's not so hard because their eye is on a larger reward.

Note: What is our heart's desire? What is our treasure? Where will our acquisitions be when we are gone? What example are we setting for others to follow? If our most important activity is to chase after more stuff, we will never have enough.

THE STRUGGLE WITH FORGIVING

Forgiving and forgetting . . .
Can you have one without the other?
Is forgiveness granted if the forgetting is a grudging chore?
. . . if the forgetting has strings attached?
What if a tally is kept on a mental scorecard,
waiting to be recalled after another false step?
Or if others are waiting to say, "I told you so,"
when a genuine attempt at forgiving is tried
and fails because of another's deception,
leaving only embarrassment and the feeling of foolishness.

The memory of a wrongful act rides long into the night.
The hurt hangs on with a death-grip, refusing to give in,
taking on a life of its own—a living, breathing, energy-draining force.
To keep remembering a grievance is to keep it alive,
allowing it to feed and take root,
becoming a devoted companion . . . a reliable partner,
willing to go the extra mile as long as it's allowed,
giving it the control, it so desperately seeks.

To let it go . . . to cut it loose . . .
Isn't this the desire of the one seeking forgiveness?
    for others to show compassion,
    to have the willingness to dismiss without retribution,
    to give one the benefit of the doubt.
So, why the struggle to flip it around?
    to give when it is known how it feels to seek,

to give to others the forgiveness that has been sought.

Forgiving and forgetting . . .
Individuals struggle . . . cultures struggle . . . humanity struggles
with this concept of mercy and reprieve,
but . . . God knows the heart and mind of those who are seeking.
He is ready and willing to forgive . . . and forget.

Note: It is far easier to ask for forgiveness than grant forgiveness. I was thinking how hard it is for people to let go when they have been wronged in some way even though they have been guilty of wrongdoing themselves. We are called to forgive and love each other.

KEEPING IT SIMPLE

She began to grow on him.
Seeing her began to make his heart skip a beat,
maybe even do a little dance.

He thought he could see a hint of attraction in her eyes,
a slight smile on her face,
but they were both too shy to take the first step.

Emissaries had to intervene on their behalf,
feeling out for the other's intent,
trying to discover a glimmer of what could be.

He was supposed to be calm and cool, a self-assured adult,
but his memory conjured up a picture of a nervous second grader,
exploring a first crush on the playground at recess.

He remembered sending a note with a friend.
A simple note: I like you. Do you like me?
A box was drawn beside the word yes . . . a box beside no.

It was agonizing waiting for an answer.
What would it be?
Could he handle a check beside no?

His buddy came running back,
handing him the note—his hands shaking—
afraid to see which box was checked.

He faintly remembered his heart racing
as he stared at the paper in his hands,
seeing a big check mark beside . . . yes.

This scene flashed before his mind's eye
as he nervously approached her from across the room.
Nothing registered as to what he would say.

Their eyes locked on each other.
A trace of a smile came across her face.
It was time to open his mouth and talk.

Beginnings don't have to be difficult; keep it simple.
Simple greetings . . . simple conversations.
Simple innocence . . . just like second grade.

His mouth was dry—his tongue paralyzed.
Finally, "Hi" came out of his mouth.
"Hi" came out of hers.

Note: I was thinking about how, as adults, we overcomplicate meetings. Just have simple conversations about simple things. This is how friendship can begin.

STORM

The clouds are darkening in the west,
the storm beginning to build,
heading this way, ready to unleash its impending fury.
Flashes of lightning enter nature's drama,
appearing against the bluish-black backdrop,
a not-so-subtle reminder of nature's raw power.
Thunder can now be heard.
The wind begins to surge, like incoming ocean waves—
    relentlessly pounding the shore.
Trees begin to sway; leaves come tumbling down the street,
    as if trying to outrun what is coming.
The first drops make their splatting sound
    as they strike the streets and sidewalks.
The tempo of the drops quickens
    until the individual drops can no longer be distinguished.
Their sound becomes a roar while the thunder becomes the chorus
    of the storm's deafening symphony.
The limbs of the trees are whipping back and forth violently,
as if some giant, invisible hand is shaking them,
determined to uproot them like some unwanted weed.
The streets have become raging rivers,
straining to jump their concrete banks,
rebelling against their forced containment,
craving the freedom to flow unconstrained.

The storm is waging war on everything in its path,
lashing out at all that would resist its force,

making its statement of wrath against all who would hear,

reminding us we are puny and insignificant,

leaving us awestruck in its wake.

The wind begins to die down . . .

The trees begin to still . . .

Leaves have ceased their race.

The temporary street rivers have begun to ebb.

The bluish-black sky is replaced by one of blue.

Birds begin to sing their songs.

Life begins to settle back into its normal rhythms.

All that is left is a remnant of nature's angry outburst,

its fury purged for the moment,

its soul cleansed and refreshed,

its beauty placed back on display in the aftermath.

A rainbow can be seen arcing across the sky,

almost as if Mother Nature is offering an apology for her angry outburst.

Note: The fury of nature is an awesome and fearsome sight to behold but also a welcome window into the beauty of God's creation.

SILENT COMFORT

The lightning storm was in full swing,
bolts lighting up the sky with their jagged brilliance,
some seeming to freeze for seconds.
Nature's fireworks were on display,
temporarily turning night into day,
with thunder providing the soundtrack to complete the show—
at times rattling the windows for extra emphasis.

I was uneasy from the storm;
memories from my youth crept back,
memories of fear and anxiety.
As an adult, I knew the science behind it all,
but my jitters were still triggered all the same.
My heart beat a little faster,
my breathing . . . not quite as calm.

My five-year old daughter came into my bedroom,
her sleep disturbed by the weather display.
She was clearly unsettled,
her eyes glistening, on the verge of tears,
hugging her rabbit for comfort.
Her silent request was obvious.
I motioned for her, and she jumped in the bed.

Nothing was said as I wrapped her in my arms.
We sensed the unease in each other
and drew comfort in one another's presence.

Before long, she was breathing deeply;

the security of my embrace had chased her demons away.

Little did my daughter know, as she slept peacefully . . .

she had done the same for me.

Note: This scene came to mind as I was riding out a severe thunderstorm. There is nothing as sacred as the safety and well-being of our children.

SIMPLE THERAPY

Sunshine and fresh air—
    the warmth on my face;
    the soft caress of the breeze—
both relaxing with their invisible touch,
both soothing on my skin.

The feel reminded me of clean sheets off the clothesline
after hours spent fluttering in the breeze,
purified by sun and air,
before being retrieved by my mother.
The scent of clean was distinct in my nose
as I would climb under them,
my body at rest after a long day of play.
I would breathe deeply . . . inhaling the smell;
it was a good smell,
reminding me of the care she took
with her tasks to take care of us all.

Fresh air and sunshine—
    both awakening my spirit,
    lifting it upward to the heavens—
their restorative powers,
cleansing . . . renewing . . . healing.

Note: Sometimes, it's the simple things that can offer the greatest amount of healing, renewing our spirit in a time of depression.

SNOW

A snow-covered morning is quite beautiful,
the sun reflecting off the pure white blanket,
grass snuggled underneath,
the fluffy powder resting in slight swells
like those on a lake, only frozen in place,
its surface smooth before it is marred by human activity,
the snow masking any imperfections hiding underneath.

Snow is unusual for this clime;
a light coating of two to four inches will occur on occasion,
school-age kids hoping for a "snow day" to miss school.
This week was one for the record books—
    first time ever—windchill warning, as low as 30 below,
    temperature reaching two-below zero on Tuesday,
    another storm blowing in the next day,
    power outages everywhere,
    people hunkered down, trying to stay warm—
    in some cases, trying to just stay alive,
    water systems failing—water boil advisories issued
    (Even the Valley is stricken by the cold).
Anger is rising—questions go unanswered.
The weather is temporary;
the aftermath? not so much.

The snow is still beautiful.
It is the byproduct of the elements,
wished for by children and adults alike—

     to gaze at,

     to revel in,

     to make memories in.

Sometimes wishes are granted, so be careful when wishing.

Don't blame the snow for this quandary.

You can't have one without the other.

Blame the cold; snow is just its every-now-and-then gift.

Note: This is my take on SNOVID in Texas, 2021.

A NEW LOOK AT MONDAY

Look at a calendar: Sunday is the first day, not Monday.
Biblically: Sunday is the seventh day—meant for rest.
Realistically: Monday is the first day—the dreaded beginning.

Why does Monday get such a bad rap?
Do we play so hard on the weekends that Monday has become a day to recover—
    maybe even a day of rest;
or the beginning of something to be approached with apprehension—
    students going back to school, learning lessons
        which they deem unnecessary,
        which tax and try them,
        which make them long for a life after school;
    adults going to work at a job to be endured—not enjoyed—longing for the carefree days of retirement when they can just sit and rest;
    elderly seniors, who have graduated to the last phase of life, wishing for the routine
        of school or work, forgetting that both were disliked . . . maybe even detested.
This emotional trap, in which we find ourselves entangled,
    weighs on us . . .
        drains us . . .
            discourages us . . .

Consideration: Let Monday be the launchpad for what is possible.

Begin the week in prayer and thankfulness.
Begin the week with a smile and a spirit of anticipation.

Begin the week chasing your dreams and helping others chase theirs.

Begin the week with the idea of learning something new.

Begin the week uplifting others who view Monday with . . . dread.

Note: It is time to take a new look on how we begin a week or any day which we have been given, a day to seek out all that is possible.

THE REWARD OF IMPATIENCE

Hurry, hurry, hurry.
Rush, rush, rush.
Always in a hurry.
Always in a rush.

When at the end,
what has been missed?
from all the hurry, hurry, hurry;
from all the rush, rush, rush.

It can't be rewound.
It can't be freeze-framed.
Once it's gone,
it's forever gone.

The remorse is painful,
felt deep within.
It's never in a hurry.
It's never in a rush.

When at the end,
regret is sadly felt—
from all the hurry, hurry, hurry;
from all the rush, rush, rush.

Note: This can apply to a lifetime or a day. Impatience always aids in setting up the domino chain of failure just waiting for the first to tip over. The resulting chain reaction is always a helpless feeling and never welcome.

A TRUE FRIEND . . .

will laugh with you
will celebrate with you
will suffer with you
will cry with you
will stand by you
will listen to you
will . . . if asked, advise you
will uplift you . . . if needed, carry you
will hold you accountable . . . if needed, challenge you
will forgive you

Will you . . . reciprocate?

Note: Just thinking about what true friendship should look like. Sadly, it doesn't always work out like it should.

AGAINST THE ODDS

The gnarled and twisted cedar appeared to sprout from the rock,
its beginning emanating long ago from a seed,
which had somehow nestled in a crack.
Day after day it must have fought for existence,
shooting its roots deep into the fissure in which it was embedded,
searching for any moisture upon which it could drink,
slowly gaining a toehold in the crevice,
widening it little . . . by . . . little,
forcing its way into what soil it could find,
willing the ground to yield to its tenacity,
to accept its presence in a rugged and unforgiving environment.
The strength of the cedar was hidden underneath,
the roots latching on with a fierce relentlessness,
allowing the old cedar to withstand the elements
which were trying to vanquish it from this rocky realm.
It stood in defiance of the odds pitted against its existence,
its survival the epitome of perseverance.
Is there a lesson in its story?

Note: I have always been amazed at the tenacity of nature.

THE EDGE OF CHOICE

Memory is a fickle thing,
selected snippets of what is desired—
    some recalled fondly, strengthening bonds with the past;
    some with harsh recollections, strengthening resentment of perceived
    wrongs.
It is a two-edged sword which cuts both ways,
manipulating our emotions to suit its whims.
Those snippets can be directed at the same person on any given day.
Such is the power of selective memory;
whether used as a weapon, striking out with wrathful retribution,
or a protective stroke, defending what is beloved and cherished,
depends on which edge of the sword is chosen.

Note: What we choose to remember and how we choose to remember can trigger a variety of emotions. Memories can cut deeply when recalled—from nostalgic longing to angry payback.

ONE SPARK

The wood was gathered.
Sticks and branches of varying sizes
    were placed around the stone ring in stacks,
ready to be used to build the fire.
But the wood couldn't be placed with random whimsy
    if the fire was to provide warmth . . .
    if the fire was to provide comfort . . .
    if the fire was to last . . .
The smaller pieces would be used to start the blaze,
placed under the pyramid structure of the larger.
If the preparation was done well,
the small tinder would ignite easily—
providing the flame to set the pyramid ablaze.
Extra wood would be used to fuel the fire through the evening,
allowing the fire to maintain itself,
the elements working in concert to provide what was intended,
but even though everything is ready and in place,
the fire can't start without a source of flame to put it all in motion.
Remember . . . it just takes one spark.

Note: Everything can be planned and in place but one "something" is still needed to put events in motion with all working together to maintain the momentum of the start.

CINDERELLA WAS A BEAR

The party had lasted for three weeks,
the celebration held in the confines of a bubble,
ending a most unusual season.
Sixty-eight had all come dressed in their best.
For some, it was an annual event.
For others, it was their inaugural trip—
    their eyes filled with wonder and awe,
        determined to enjoy the gala for as long as they could,
        never knowing if this would be their last invite.
One final act was left in this most anticipated of events.
The last two left had withstood the tests thrown their way
    and stood facing each other to claim the prize on the final night.
Their arrival on this last night was no surprise.
The prognosticators from across the land had looked into their crystal ball
    and forecast this pairing.
They were also unanimous in the outcome's prediction:
    Cinderella was expected to leave the party before midnight . . .
    disappointed.
One problem—Cinderella showed up to the party as a Bear
    and wasn't wearing glass slippers.
From the outset, it was clear who would wear the crown,
leaving no doubt in any attendee's mind who was the best.
Cinderella had won the day—dressed in green and gold—
staying at the party well past midnight, celebrating the coronation of a
champion.

Note: I wrote this in response to Baylor's victory over Gonzaga in the 2021 National Championship game. It was a great day for all Bear fans.

A CHAMPION'S HEART

To lay it all on the line and have nothing left at the end
To commit and strive with relentless vigor
To put heart and soul into the pursuit of a mission
To subject willingly to the scrutiny of the crowd
> while turning a deaf ear to the critics and naysayers
To face a formidable opponent and not flinch
To make no apologies or excuses for a failed outcome
To be gracious in defeat and humble when victorious
To keep attempting what seems impossible and find joy in the challenge
To have these attributes is to discover the heart of a champion beating within

Note: I wrote this after watching the National Championship game between Gonzaga and Baylor in 2021. Both teams demonstrated grit and determination to achieve their goal. The sportsmanship and demeanor of both was refreshing to watch. Both squads truly displayed a champion's heart.

SOONER OR LATER

The promotion had come, the result of hard work,
of years of movement through the ranks,
successful navigation through the new challenges.
Extra hours had been logged to earn the chance.
His performance had been impressive to this point,
marked by the promise of things to come—
> ready for the test,
> ready to run the gauntlet,
> ready to blaze a new trail.
Would the rise continue? or stall in its tracks?
No matter the level of confidence, a sliver of doubt exists
somewhere in the recesses of the psyche,
waiting to bolster self-doubt unless it's quashed.
The initial days will determine if success is to continue
or if the rise has reached the dreaded . . . level of incompetence.
The line between success and failure or mediocrity is razor thin.
A delicate balancing act ensues daily, the self-imposed pressure builds.
The need for success, to prove to others that the job is not too big,
that the correct decision was made, the promotion justified.
Some might ask,
> why be subject to the added pressure?
> why be prone to the incessant demands to perform?
> why not remain in the background and let others take the heat?
> why not play it safe?
They don't understand
> the drive to excel,
> the need to jump into the fray,

the desire to test the limits.

Is it better to have risked it all and fail?

or sit on the side and watch, never having risked anything?

Sooner or later . . . this decision must be faced.

Note: This scene plays out every day somewhere. I applaud those who are willing to take the risk to discover what they are capable of achieving even to the point of failing. We will always be left wondering if we don't try.

DEAR VINCENT

If only you could have known the joy your work brings.
If only you could have known the acclaim your work now receives.
If only you could have known the acceptance of your peers,
    for it is now accepted universally as genius.
If only you could have known peace in your lifetime.
If only you could have somehow erased your tortured spirit.
If only . . . if only . . . if only.

Maybe you knew you were ahead of your time.
Maybe you knew your work would one day be accepted.
Maybe you knew your time would be short,
    so you drove yourself with a maddening frenzy to the very edge of the
    cliff and . . . off.
Maybe you knew the finished work was the only way to ease your pain—
    to capture what your eyes had seen in the way only you could see it.
In that moment, maybe you knew the peace which you sought.
Was your final act because you felt you had no more to give?

I celebrate your work—what you left for us to behold.
You took the risk to pave the way for others to follow.
I look at your "Starry Nights" and am transfixed in place.
Painted on the canvas is the beauty of the night as you saw it,
    frozen for all to see it in the same way,
    to view the world through your eyes.
Is this what you intended all along?

Note: I was looking at pictures of Van Gogh's paintings and wrote this as a letter to his troubled spirit.

BEAUTY STEPPING OUT

I could see her approaching through the mist.
She seemed to be floating as if the mist were a cloud
and she, a passenger from some heavenly realm.
Her image, unfocused as if she were an apparition in a dream,
gave the appearance of elegance and grace,
heightening my anticipation,
giving me the slightest hint of what could be.

The little that I see is a tease . . . a flirtation . . . a seduction.
Was she real or some spectral illusion?
Would her beauty match the vision beginning to take shape in my mind?
Would it be better to hold on to that dream of what could be?
or embrace what is emerging, embrace what is becoming real?
It's as if she is trying to step out of the painting into reality,
leaving her world and joining me . . . in mine—
the essence of beauty coming out, of beauty being born.

Note: I was looking at an image online, and this poem is the result. The anticipation of something can sometimes leave us disappointed when the something actually occurs . . . but then . . . sometimes not.

UNEXPECTED BEAUTY

I grabbed the old metal pail,
its rust-covered, metal skin a visual testimony
of its losing battle with time and the elements.
It wasn't much to look at but still served its purpose.
I rushed to fill the old container at the hydrant;
water was sloshing and swirling within as I hurried along.

My mind was a thousand miles away
when my eye caught a glimpse of reflected light,
registering a flash of brilliant color below the translucent surface.
I noticed softening shades of yellow and orange,
appearing in alternating crescents;
the shades reminiscent of rich butter and ripe melons.
Rings of turquoise were intersecting the arcs.
Shades of brown and blue and green were hiding under shadows.
The light reflected from the surface pinwheeled to a vortex off-center.
The sides of the pail had become contrasting shades
of orange and brown, intermingled to display a richness of color,
doing its best to imitate the arboreal foliage as seen on a New England fall day.

I am sure that what I was seeing could be explained
by the physical properties of light—reflection, refraction, diffusion . . .
But wouldn't that take away from the wonder and magic of the moment?
from the mystery of the transformation of ordinary into beautiful?
I chose to not question the how or the why
but to simply enjoy the surprise of finding beauty in an unexpected place.

Note: Be observant. One never knows when or where beauty can be found.

THANK YOU, CLAUDE

I know what I like and what I don't.
I am lacking when it comes to my knowledge of art—
　　impressionism, cubism, expressionism, surrealism . . .
For me, it all runs together.
I just look at the painting and see what I see,
but I can appreciate what is before my eyes,
　　the time-consuming work,
　　the many strokes of a brush,
　　the blending of color,
　　the passion that went into the work.
I don't know why a painting is considered a masterpiece,
but I'm not compelled to know the why.
I just know what I like when I see it.

My eye has always been drawn to Monet's work.
The dreamlike quality draws me in—
　　the blurred images,
　　the indistinct edges,
　　the various hues appearing to melt on the canvas.
It's like trying to bring a dream into focus.
The images seem just out of reach behind a diaphanous veil.
They sooth and calm and draw me in,
my eye constantly searching for the details barely hidden from view.

Thank you, Claude, for your tireless effort—
　　to constantly work and rework the shades of color,
　　　　influenced by the changing seasons and light;

to work with the landscapes of your garden,
    allowing me to view and appreciate the subtleties of those changes.
Thank you for creating a living laboratory to aid in your work,
giving me a window into your world and to see it with your eyes.
Thank you for a lifelong commitment to your art,
so we might enjoy the fruits of your passionate labor.
Humanity is the beneficiary . . . the recipient of your gift.

Note: I love looking at Monet's work. This is my tribute to him and the joy his work brings to me.

GOODBYE, LARRY

The news of your passing gave me pause.
I remembered the pleasure you gave me
    as I rode the trail with Gus and Call,
    as I explored the unknown West with the Berrybenders,
    as I laughed out loud and cried with Sonny and Duane
        and their experiences of youthful angst,
    as I watched Duane go through the stages of life
        until his passing,
    as I experienced the comedies and misadventures
        of a collection of oddball characters
        whose lives were much closer to real than not,
        giving me comfort that maybe I'm not so off-center,
    as I read of your experiences in Hollywood,
    as I read of your small-town roots,
        giving us common ground upon which to tread,
    as I read your unique perspective on all things Texas,
        which ruffled a few feathers in your home state,
        but you never flinched—
            maybe even wearing the badge of curmudgeon with honor
            and aplomb.
I am sad that no new words will come forth from your pen,
but I am glad I can revisit your work at my leisure,
experiencing all over again the broad range of emotions which your words
summon.
Goodbye, Larry.
I will miss you.

Note: This is my goodbye to one of my favorite authors, Larry McMurtry, a fellow Texan.

"HOWDY, FOLKS"

"Howdy, folks. Welcome to the State Fair of Texas."
Big Tex gives his iconic welcome,
ringing out from high above the fair-grounds
to all who would attend this annual affair.
This year he is welcoming back fair-goers after a year off—
 he too falling victim to COVID in 2020.
The excitement for this year's opening is building . . . growing.
All are eagerly anticipating the vast array of sights, sounds, and smells—
 an all-out assault on the senses,
  twenty-four days to experience all this event has to offer.

The Midway is filled with games,
the thrill of winning an oversized prize enticing participation.
Rides for all ages are awaiting -
 rides which twist, turn, drop, swing, twirl—
sometimes leaving riders gasping for breath
or with a sick feeling in the pit of their stomach
but still wanting to repeat the experience.
Food booths are intermingled throughout,
positioned so no one has to walk far to satisfy their craving,
appealing to the appetites of young and old alike,
offering the typical fare and many surprises—
 batter-dipped and fried, both savory and sweet.
If it can be dipped, it can be fried—
 Snickers, butter, coke, pizza, pecan pie, bacon, Oreos, S'mores . . .
but the king of all these foods is found at the feet of Big Tex.
Fletcher's Corny Dog has ruled supreme for decades—

pierce a wiener with a stick;

dip it in a cornmeal batter;

fry it until golden brown;

slather it in mustard.

The sensory pleasure begins with the first bite.

It's something that has to be experienced to understand.

Remorse begins to settle in as the corny dog disappears,

leaving one desirous of one more crunchy bite.

The newest offerings in cars and trucks are on display,

beckoning all to sit in and experience that "new car" smell,

day dreaming of driving off in the vehicle of their choice.

Pavilions full of wares and gadgets for sale are waiting,

with demonstrations designed to show the necessity,

hawkers insistent, "No home should be without."

The prize-winners of all types of crafts are ready to be viewed—

all works of art in their own right—

from quilts pieced together with care and skill to paintings and photographs.

Cooking and baking contests are scheduled throughout,

the smells and aromas replacing Pavlov's bell.

Livestock are waiting to be shown and grand champions named,

giving their owners reason to preen and strut.

Attendees leave exhausted by the end of the day,

many children asleep with their head on a parent's shoulder,

balloons attached to their tiny wrists,

the faint trace of a smile left on their face.

Memories have been made to add to the memories from previous years.

The countdown of days for next year has already begun,

the memory bank anticipating more additions for years to come.

As they leave, Big Tex is still calling from 55 feet above the ground, "Howdy, folks."

His words of welcome, heard at the start of the day,

have become a reminder as they walk into the night,

"Don't be a stranger and come again."

Note: The State Fair of Texas is the largest of its kind. It is an event that must be experienced. Words to adequately describe all that happens within the fair-grounds are difficult to script. It is sensory-overload waiting to happen.

TECHNO LIFE

The network is down.
The WiFi isn't working.
I can't get a signal.
I am trapped in a tecno-crazed world—
    dependence on devices, like an out-of-control addiction;
    must be connected if life is to carry on;
    stifled and paralyzed when not connected.

Information is retrieved with lightning speed.
Transactions are made with the push of a key.
We surf along on an internet stream,
    riding the wave with confidence until the stream is broken—
    wiping out the result—
    leaving us wringing our hands in alarm.

Some remember when connected was a landline hooked to a rotary dial;
    or television reception from an antenna;
    or music via a transistor radio.

Is being dependent on all these techno-devices . . . an advancement?
Is being handcuffed by that dependence . . . an advancement?
Is the human element being reduced . . . an advancement?
Are we busy planning our own obsolescence? our own demise?

What was once considered a movie fantasyland,
    a world confined to images projected onto the silver screen,
    is fast becoming our reality . . . our virtual existence.

Will we one day awaken and find ourselves trapped inside a "high-def" video game?

　　our life being manipulated by some unseen operator, subject to its whims.

When we believe we can't live without all this techno razzle dazzle,

　　we will then be headed down the path to complete reliance,

　　　　a path from which there could be no return . . .

　　　　relinquishing all control . . .

　　　　　　taking the final step through the screen into the virtual game.

Note: I can't help thinking these thoughts when I see people attached to their phones and the helpless look on their face when they can't get a signal; or how agitated we become when the cable is out and television programming comes to a grinding halt; or how desperate we become when computer systems are down and data can't be retrieved; or how . . . I think you see where I am going with this.

THE ROAD BACK TO SIMPLE

It was a time envisioned in black and white—
    television, movies, newsprint, photographs, decisions.
It was a time which was simpler, not as complex—
    yes or no sufficed;
    "maybe" didn't exist.
Shades of gray were seen but ignored.
It was best to keep things uncomplicated.

When gray entered the drama,
when the transition was recognized,
it clouded the view, muddled the scene.
Answers weren't as clear cut.
Answers had become vague.
Decisions were questioned and debated.
The black and white way of thinking began to quiz their gray counterparts:
    why all the fuss?
    why the questions?
    why ask . . . why?
The response to all:
    why not?

The technicolor world threw everything into disarray.
The forgone time of black and white was in absolute shock,
leaving it full of questions and mind-numbing doubts.
Even the grays didn't know what to do or say.
The vibrant world of color called everything into question—
    nothing was sacred;

nothing was unchallenged;

nothing was safe from scrutiny.

It was all turned upside down and inside out.

All was laid bare, as naked as a newborn babe,

exposed for all to see and inspect,

to pass judgement,

to liberate what was deemed outdated and useless,

implementing its own code of what should and should not be.

The answers were whatever seemed right in the moment—

maybe, yes;

maybe, no;

maybe . . . maybe?

Questions:

Who has the answers?

What now?

Where to go from here?

When will the madness end?

Why all the turmoil?

Different hues are formed by swirling and mixing.

A deft touch is required to find the right shade,

to lighten or darken, finding the desired tint.

But . . . sometimes simple is still desired;

sometimes the answers are still black and white, not . . . maybe—

yes, to kindness—no to cruelty;

yes, to courtesy—no to rudeness;

yes, to empathy—no to indifference;

yes, to love—no to contempt.

For these . . . there is no debate.

Note: So many times, we make our lives complicated when it can really be simple and uncomplicated.

STEREOTYPES

Why the compulsion to categorize, to pigeonhole,
sorting by gender or race or occupation or religion or . . .
Does it bring some kind of comfort?
Is it a way to validate our suspicions and fears?
Does it elevate our own self-esteem?
    allowing us to walk a little more upright,
    to walk with more of a spring in our step.
Is the price tag the demeaning of those who are different?

We have stuffed others into various pigeonholes until they are overflowing,
but our own complaints ring loudly
    when we find ourselves in some overcrowded little cubby,
    shoulder to shoulder with others who have been deemed . . . the same.
We all try to crawl out of these tight spaces,
struggling to carve out room in this judgmental world,
crying out to be judged on our own merits—
    not by some set of preconceived notions.
We claim our own God-given uniqueness
    while doubting that same uniqueness in others.

Don't we all hope and dream?
Don't we all laugh and cry?
Don't we all feel sorrow and pain?
Don't we all long for safety and security?
Don't we all desire a better world for our children?
    a world free from this need to classify.

Oh, if only . . . if only we could realize we are far more similar than different.

Note: Is this dream too big to be realized? The year of COVID has exposed many fears and suspicions which exist just below the surface of our societal mindset.

DRAWN BY HOPE

Poverty . . . violence . . . oppression . . . COVID.
Not the four horsemen, but at least close cousins,
sucking out the last vestiges of hope.
Despair is digging in, refusing to let go,
body and soul beaten down,
ready to be counted out—
until . . . a whisper of a rumor can be heard:
welcoming arms await, willing to take them in.

Hope is rekindled from dying embers, born from desperation.
A glimmer, even though faint, is better than nothing,
better than a darkness completely devoid of light,
better than waiting for the final crushing blow,
ending their existence and that of their children—
the chance of a new life . . . a chance of new beginnings.
The rumor is a siren's call beckoning them to come

Families begin their northward march . . . step by step.
Some send only children in the care of older children.
Each step brings them closer to their destination.
Hope's glimmer burns a little brighter.
They carry what they can and leave the rest,
with no thought of returning, only pressing forward,
like an ant trail stretching into eternity.

The final steps of their journey reach the Rio Bravo;
on the other side lies the land where the rumor was born,

the land resonating hope, singing of opportunity.
Some have family already here.
Most have no one waiting, but still they come,
their numbers increasing day by day.
Hope is a powerful magnet drawing all to its breast,
filling each with the promise of something better, something finer.

They cross the river to holding stations,
uncertainty of what to expect creeps in.
They have become unwitting pawns in a political chess match.
Both sides in the match are pointing an accusatory finger of blame.
The media is circling and questioning.
Is the honeymoon over for the newly elected?
Their opponent is trying to recapture what was lost,
using these events to their advantage, crying outrage,
but neither side knows what to do.
All the while, these new arrivals sit and wait—
 still believing in the rumor which started the quest;
 still believing in hope's sweet song, even though faint;
 still believing in the dream of a transcendent future
  for their children and their children's children.
They close their eyes and feel the beat of hope's heart.

Note: I wrote this after watching several reports on the National News about the great migration from Central America in 2021 by those seeking refuge within our borders.

ALWAYS REMEMBER

9/11, two numbers said together which recall so much—
    the open-mouthed shock of disbelief,
    the horror of the destruction and death,
    the emotional devastation showered on a watching nation,
    the tearful anguish of those suffering loss,
    the wrathful anger calling for swift retribution.
It sends out a 9-1-1 call for us to always remember.
We view the photographs and images of the event,
    detailing the dust-covered individuals seeking shelter,
    detailing the emotional trauma of the survivors,
    detailing the grim determination of first-responders rendering aid.
The faces are frozen in time, some remaining forever young.
None of them will ever see another birthday, another anniversary.
They will never experience another family gathering during holiday seasons.
They will never again experience the joy of a loving embrace.
They will never know the how or why of their demise.

This infamous date is this generation's Pearl Harbor.
Now, as then, they are both testimonies to the unshakable resilience
and the unflappable resolve
    of a people unwilling to give in to fear,
    of a people unified in their purpose to give comfort and aid,
    of a people with a steadfast spirit, undeterred by a terroristic threat,
    of a people who are not defined by their symbols alone,
    of a people ready to look the enemy in the eye and rise to the challenge,
    of a people ready to defend this proud nation with its last breath
    against any who would attack these shores.

The monuments we have built—

> one in a field in Pennsylvania, commemorating those brave souls
> who saved thousands with their sacrifice,

> the other filling the void left by the twin towers which once reached
> to the sky,

> both filled with the engraved names of those who perished—

call upon us to never forget the tragedy.

They call on us to remain vigilant against those with misguided ideologies,
both at home and abroad, who would attack our way of life.

They call on us to protect those who cannot protect themselves.

They call on us to remember that with freedom comes sacrifice.

They call on us to never forget the unity on display in the tragedy's
aftermath,

> remembering what we can do together . . .

> remembering what we can become when we join as one . . .

Our lasting tribute is to never let their deaths be in vain, to always
remember.

Note: The images on TV of the 20th anniversary of 9/11 brought back the shock and horror of that day. It reminded me that there are those who would destroy what we, in this nation, hold dear. It reminded me we must be ever vigilant in our resolve to protect our freedoms. What saddens me is that it takes tragedy for us to set aside our differences and bring us together.

STAND WITH ME

I stand as freedom's symbol,
    raising my torch for all to see,
    looking out over the ocean waves,
    beckoning to all who would come,
    to all searching for opportunity.
They still come to our shores filled with hope,
    buoyed by the promise of what this land can provide,
    but not all in this land welcome those who would come.
Fear and suspicion weigh them down.
They have forgotten their forefathers were once greeted by me,
    were welcomed by me when they first traveled to our shores.

I am a symbol of what could be;
I am a symbol of equality;
I am a symbol of fairness;
I am a symbol of protection.
I not only stand as a beacon to those who would come
    but also, for those who are already here.
Embrace the ideals for which I stand—
    for what is decent and good in the human spirit,
    for all the possibilities which can be realized.
I am Lady Liberty. Stand with me.

Note: People tend to forget how blessed this country has been throughout its history. No matter how many problems we think we have, people still look to our nation as a beacon of hope in a troubled world.

THE CHILD WHO WILL NEVER KNOW

The scene was like something from *The Star-Spangled Banner*:
 "... the rocket's red glare, the bombs bursting in air ..."
The white trails of the rockets were tracing across the sky,
met by their counterparts in midair,
resulting in an explosive show for all to see.
If this was in July, and almost half a world away,
it would be mistaken for a fireworks extravaganza,
lighting up the night sky,
a way to celebrate the birth of a nation,
children joyously watching the colorful display.
But this was not a celebration ... this was real ... this was anger run amuck,
fueled by a centuries old conflict,
innocents on both sides caught in the crossfire.
There was no joy or thrill in their eyes ... only terror and fear.
The children here were watching the arc of death,
   shivering in shelters ...
   crying for protection from those gathered around ...
   asking, why is this happening ...
   wondering if they would see the sun rise tomorrow ...

What does a child know of competing ideologies?
What does a child know of hatred, unless it is taught by adults?
What about the child who will never know what it is like
   to experience love's first kiss,
   to experience the events of growing up,
   to experience the birth of their own children
because an adult chose to press a button, unleashing destruction,

sending death racing across the sky for a preemptive strike on hopes and dreams.

Note: This was written in response to the missile attacks between Hamas and Israel. The images on TV of children huddled with their parents in bomb shelters saddened and horrified me. Children should never be put in harm's way by adults who cannot resolve their differences in a peaceful manner.

WHAT WILL HAPPEN TO HER NOW?

Her world was torn apart, in total disarray.
The dreams she had, of what she wanted from life,
were now in doubt . . . were fleeing from her.
She could never be swift enough to catch them,
to grab hold and let them carry her away from this turmoil.
Would her longing to be viewed as more that an object—
        a piece of property, something to be traded, a bartering chip—
be swept away like dust in the wind?
Would her desire to be considered an equal be smitten and beaten down?
Would her voice, which had just begun to be heard, be silenced?
Would she now be a visible outcast in this new world?
pushed into a corner—seen but not heard.
The haunted look in her eyes tells a story,
a story where hope has been ripped away,
leaving despair in its place.
So . . . what will happen to her now?

Note: The recent overthrow of the government in Afghanistan got me to thinking about the plight of women in this area of the world, but this has been a recurring theme throughout the course of time. Women have been devalued down through the centuries. Theirs is a constant struggle to be heard, accepted, and appreciated in a male-dominated society.

THE FRONTLINE

They walk through the door.
Another day begins
    where hope is in short supply,
    where feeling helpless and powerless is the norm,
    where death is an anticipated companion.
Time is dragging in slow-motion, sometimes in stop-action,
    wishing that the fast forward button could be pressed.
Months of extra shifts have been logged,
    tirelessly working against the odds—
    overworked and understaffed, but doing their best.
Some are called out of retirement to lend a hand.
Casualties are incurred within their own ranks.

The eyes reveal a somber story.
Their haunted look tells of fatigue, desperation, depression, dejection . . .
Ghosts walk the hallways, searching for a way back, a way home.
There is not time to process one death before another occurs.
They fall on a couch for some much-needed sleep,
    thrashing about restlessly with scenes of death floating through their
    mind.
They awaken to continue their walking nightmare.
Some are on the verge of mental collapse, wondering if they could be the
next casualty.
They carry on with grim determination because there is no other choice.

With enough time, this pandemic shall pass.
The record of its devastation will be etched in the chronicles of time.
With enough time, the experience will fade like a distant echo.

But for those who worked on the frontline . . .

will there ever be enough time to erase the memory of death?

Note: The images of overworked hospital staff during the new surge of the delta variant painted a startling picture of those who continue to live the nightmare but battle through their fatigue and fear to help those who come through the doors. So much of this could have been prevented.

KNOCKING AT THE DOOR

I am here, the new kid, third cousin of the OG.
I am finding new and fertile fields in which I can grow,
establishing my roots before destruction can reach me,
while others refuse to listen on how to prevent my spread.

You have tried to ignore the warnings of my arrival.
Your stubborn streak . . . or indecisiveness (take your pick),
has given me an open invitation to plant my seed,
allowing me to patiently wait until the time of harvest.

You can run, but you can't hide.
I am crueler and more unforgiving than my cousins.
You will never see me coming,
so don't be shocked when I knock at your door.

Note: The news keeps chronicling the spread of the new variant among the unvaccinated
in the population and how aggressive it is. Some people seem remorseful about their
delay in getting the vaccine while others keep displaying outright disregard at the urgings
of the health care professionals who are tracking the spread of this virus. Their refusal
to believe and follow the recommendations being given has left me shaking my head in
wonder. Only when the virus strikes at their doorstep, do they begin to take the news
seriously. By then, it could be too late.

I'M SO SORRY

Why must I wear a mask?
Why is my child being mandated to wear a mask?
Why am I being encouraged to be vaccinated?
Isn't all of this my choice?
What happened to my freedom and liberty?

I rail against these intrusions.
I shout out with anger and frustration.
Leave me alone, and let me live my life.
I protest against my inability to choose for my child.
I know what is best for me and mine.

I now have the symptoms.
Will I pass it on?
Is my family safe?
Why didn't I listen?
Why did I ignore the imploring of others?

I have now become a statistic,
another unvaccinated testing positive,
claiming another bed in an overwhelmed setting.
I am now isolated from my family,
fearing for their safety . . . I'm so sorry I didn't listen.

Note: With the rapid spread of the Delta variant, the unvaccinated who are being hospitalized are imploring others to get vaccinated. They are expressing sorrow and regret for failing to heed the advice of health officials. Deaths are beginning to pile up once again. The words, "I'm so sorry I didn't get vaccinated," keep ringing out on the news telecasts. There will be people who will still not listen to this pleading cry of remorse.

THE MESSAGE OF SILENCE

The hateful words of unjustified criticism came spewing forth—
words of hateful vitriol, words of malice—
their intent to inflame and agitate . . . to ridicule.
Their message was not being delivered with timidity or reservation;
it was being shouted to the heavens for all to hear,
drawing a symbolic line in the dirt,
challenging those who would oppose, to step across.
What does it say if few take up the challenge?
If they choose to ignore the rhetoric by their silence,
are they accepting this diatribe?
Are they hoping it will go away by itself with no effort on their part?
Is their silence an act of fear . . . or apathy?
Which is worse?
Is the silence unintentional validation?
Is saying nothing indulging the rantings being spouted?
Is tolerance allowing momentum to grow?
the fifteen minutes of fame increasing exponentially,
building into an unstoppable avalanche of hyperbole.
Does the "sticks and stones" adage work
when the words are pointing the finger of accusation falsely?
Does the closed mouth of those who would oppose,
leaving the critical—even hateful—words unchallenged,
make a statement just as clear and just as loud . . .
We tend to forget silence delivers its own message—
a message which is allowed to be shaped and molded by others.

Note: With all the words being shouted from all sides during this time of extreme stress, it is a delicate line we walk determining when to speak out and when to listen. When the words are being shouted from a platform of hate and ignorance, can we afford to remain silent?

REALITY SETTING IN

I tune in every night to the national news,
eagerly viewing the drama from the day's events,
amazed at what is happening across the nation
while I sit safely inside my bubble,
safe from the tempest blowing relentlessly,
safe from the waves of chaos pounding on the shores of sanity.

I don't see any wildfires in my neighborhood;
I don't see politicians squabbling in my yard;
I don't see hospital beds filled with patients,
even though the news tells me the numbers are growing;
I don't see stressed out nurses dealing with this new variant and its
aftermath;
I don't see nervous parents sending their elementary-aged students to school,
    not knowing what their fate may be.
If I don't see it, can it be happening?
Am I caught up in this changing reality?

My wife is getting text messages about friends and friends of friends
who are coming down with the new variant; some will not make it.
This new reality is beginning to set in.
It is creeping closer day by day.
I was convinced the news couldn't touch me . . . until it does.

*Note: I feel so insulated from all that is happening while I sit in my easy chair at home.
The events still seem more like a Hollywood production . . . some out-of-control disaster
film; but it is all too real . . . so real.*

WHEN

Shots shatter the stillness of the night.
The death toll continues to climb like a vine out of control.
More questions about, "Why?" are asked.

Has the ability to cope with the frustrations of life disappeared?
leaving only a gun to make the decision,
its bullets delivering their fateful message.

When will calm replace anger?
using dialogue as a tool of understanding,
replacing guns as a tool of intolerance.

When can a message of compassion and healing be voiced?
guiding those who will listen to be of one accord,
instead of harsh words used as instruments of discord.

When can reason be our tool for intervention?
instead of browbeating, demoralizing, threatening, terrorizing . . .
instead of using a gun as a means of intimidation.

When can we decide that violence isn't the solution?
when disagreements occur . . . when views are at an impasse . . .
when human life is just an obstacle to be removed.

When can a human life once again be deemed sacred?
instead of something which is readily disposable,
something to be discarded on a wrathful whim.

When will enough be enough?

When will guns no longer be considered a solution?

. . . when violence and its tools are viewed with disdain by all.

Note: I am appalled at the increased gun violence which is being reported from every corner of our society. So many have forgotten how to cope with frustration and anger, turning to violence as their first and only alternative.

SELL IT

He looked at the image in the mirror.
His thoughts,

>*What truth do I use? Whose version?*
>*Don't overthink, just sell it . . . you have to sell it.*
>*Spin it to suit your needs.*
>*Slant the words to fit the desired outcome.*
>*Don't let those media jackals rattle you.*
>*Set the public's mind at ease.*
>*Just be confident with your words,*
>*instilling an unshakable belief and faith in their message,*
>*removing all questions of doubt,*
>*easing the tension that exists any way you can.*
>*You need to show strength and resolve.*
>*Now, go out and sell it*

He saw the self-assurance for which he was searching
staring back at him . . . giving him a needed boost of confidence.
He gave the image a confirming nod.
The image nodded back.
He was ready.

He walked up to the podium,
looked at the cameras with a steady gaze
and began to speak to his audience . . .

Note: With all the political-speak coming through the television news, it is hard to know what is the truth or a slanted version of the truth. People are searching for truth to ease their mind and strengthen their resolve during this tension-spiked period in which we live. What is being said by our government leadership is being closely scrutinized by every facet of our society. It feels like trust in their ability to govern and lead is waning rapidly.

STIRRING THE ANTS

I watched the little boy eyeing the ant bed, deep in his thoughts.
He had a stick gripped loosely in his hand.
His eyes went from the tip of the stick
to the orderly trail of ants entering the mound.
He began to stir the bed,
keeping a safe distance from the angered ants.
He just continued to stir the pile and observe the result.
The more he stirred and poked, the more incensed they became,
continuing to scurry in a panic, crawling over each other,
making every effort to reclaim their disturbed settlement.

The little boy sensed my presence
and turned to look into my eyes.
I was startled by the face staring back at me;
it had the appearance of a man of seventy years or more,
his hair a comb-over mess.
He challenged my presence with an irritated gaze,
as if to say, "How dare you interrupt my play."
I was somewhat taken aback by his belligerent attitude, but asked,
"Why would you stir up the ants? They were doing nothing to you.
They were just minding their business, going about their daily task."
His reply, "Because I wanted to. Because I can."

Note: This is in response to a man using fear and anger to manipulate others because he didn't get what he wanted.

READY . . . AIM . . . FIRE

Tap into fear.
Tap into frustration.
Tap into anger.
Gather those who will blindly follow.
Point them in the right direction.
They are the bullet in the gun.
The gun is loaded and ready.
Pull the trigger.
Disaster is waiting.
Violence erupts.
Stand back, and watch.
Smile, and justify the action.
Justify the words.
Take no blame.

I think I have read about this scenario before
in some other time and place.

History is repeating.
Lessons were not learned.

Note: This is a response to the Capitol takeover on January 6, 2021. When people are frustrated and angry about their situation, they can be easily manipulated into doing things which will later cause remorse and regret.

THE ROAD TRIP

I just tweeted, "It's happening. We're doing it.
History is being made." #patriotsriseup.
We are rushing the building,
pushing down the barricades.
Don't let anything stand in the way.
I pause to take a selfie.
>   *Gotta post that later;*
>   *I look cool in my hat.*
We break the glass,
break open the doors.
People are spilling into the Capitol,
yelling for all to step aside, to get out of the way.
>   *I like yelling my commands;*
>   *what a rush.*
I stop with two buddies and pose for the security cam.
>   *They will never recognize me with my face painted;*
>   *they're just morons without a clue.*
We are all wearing matching hats and shirts
that were made special for this occasion.
>   *I really need to get some "tats,"*
>   *some ink to mark the occasion.*
I send off some texts, "Guess where I am?"
We are pounding each other's back,
encouraging each other,
bolstering our courage to continue with this patriotic struggle.
>   *I gotta post this stuff on Instagram;*
>   *I wonder how many "likes" I am going to get on YouTube;*

oh wow, teargas; not cool.

People are running everywhere, shouting,

"This is our house. Take it back."

We are surging up the stairs,

walking in offices,

looking around for memorabilia to commemorate this moment.

The man called us patriots;

we're just doing what patriots should do—what we have been told to do.

We are fighting to take our country back.

I need to post my blog ASAP.

Shots ring out.

People are being hurt.

I see groups walking around with looks of triumph,

waving their flags in defiance.

What have we done?

Have we kicked the hornet's nest?

I thought this was just going to be a fun road trip.

Note: This came to mind as I was watching video of the Capitol takeover. What could have been going through the minds of all these protesters? Did they honestly think there would be no repercussions to their actions? I couldn't help but think how some were caught up in the moment and manipulated by others.

ONE OF THE PEOPLE?

People have become disenchanted with the politics of bipartisanship,
>   neither side willing to bend or compromise—
>   "My way or the highway,"
>   "To the victors go the spoils,"
>   "Might makes right."
This philosophy has bolstered a climate of divisiveness
>   where absolute blame is directed at the other side of the aisle,
>   "They are the cause for your anguish and disgust."
It sounds like an echo reverberating back and forth—
>   less than 600 people determining the future;
>   less than 600 people whose only concern is power and prestige;
>   less than 600 people who have forgotten why they are where they are;
>   less than 600 people sitting nice and cozy in their castle on the hill.
Outside their world, people are suffering with fear and dread,
>   their circumstances stampeding out of their control.
But the "less than 600" are convinced they are doing good work, exceptional work,
>   the people's work—unless you ask the group on the other side of the aisle.
That is when the argument breaks out.

I have heard the useless rhetoric, seen the dramatic show before the camera;
>   I identify with you;
>   I am one of you;
>   I work for you;
>   I make the future bright for you.
Maybe at some time in the beginning this might have been true.

Maybe they had their finger on the pulse of the public,

but years in their federal perch on the hill

has insulated them from the reality outside their walls,

from being in touch with the people's will,

until the day frustration came smashing through the door,

sending them scurrying for any place of concealment,

hoping that pain or possibly death would not find them on this day.

For the first time, they felt the fear of the everyday person

that exists outside this symbol of our democracy—

what it is like to be black or brown,

what it is like to face the unknowns of tomorrow,

what it is like to be angry and frustrated by circumstances,

what it is like to have circumstances not in their control.

They were frightened and rightfully so.

I heard words of anger in the aftermath,

lashing out because of that fear,

angered because the fear made them uncomfortable.

Now they are in touch with the people, with their constituents.

They now feel the frustration, fear, and pain of the people they serve.

They now know how splintered society has become

when a segment will blindly follow the misguided words

of a sour and bitter man.

Maybe now, when they speak, it won't be a lot of useless rhetoric.

Maybe now they can truly identify

and remember they do work for the people of this land.

These words have been my attempt to vent and rant,

my attempt to voice my frustration,

to strike some chord of reason about the current state of affairs.

Can the "less than 600" really become one of the people and find the pulse again?

Can they now have genuine empathy and not empty words stating as much?

Or will they have short-term memory and proceed with business as usual?

Note: This is my take on the response of our congressional leaders to the Capitol takeover on January 6, 2021. They had no idea of the level of frustration of the citizenry of this nation. They got a brief taste of the fear and anger which exists in our society.

A GOOD SPOT

Consider this individual—
    inflexible in thought,
    an uncompromising nature
    only has one viewpoint—theirs,
    unwilling to listen to others,
    an opposing opinion is an attack,
    anyone who doesn't think as they do is the enemy,
    always points the finger of blame at someone else.
Is this individual from the liberal left or the conservative right?
If the answer is unclear or maybe both . . . you are in a good spot.

Note: This was written in response to all the post-election stress of 2020.

THE WEIGHT OF THE WORLD

He was an average guy in every way.
Nothing really stood out in any of his features,
but he had a special power unknown to all.
He couldn't fly;
he didn't have superhuman strength;
he couldn't outrun a speeding bullet;
he couldn't shoot or spin webs.
His power? he knew what people were thinking.
He could see the thought bubble above their head,
revealing their innermost thoughts.
To him, they looked like the characters in a comic strip.
It was as if they were thinking out loud.
Nothing was secret from his watchful eye.
It was like insider trading on Wall Street.

He didn't depend on body language for insight—
    a furrowed brow—concentration or . . . worry?
    a smile, lighting up a face—anticipation or . . . a fond remembrance?
    a brisk walking pace—running late or . . . exercise?
    tears being wiped away—sadness from loss or . . . betrayal?
There was no guesswork because the bubbles were clear.
To him, there was no such thing as a "poker face"—
    no hiding a bluff;
    no pretending to suck someone in while holding an unbeatable hand.
He could read exactly what was going through a person's mind.
Their secrets and desires, their passions, were an open book for him to read.

In the beginning, it had been intriguing, even . . . fun.

He was caught up in sharing the euphoric joy of success

and the personal celebrations of special events.

The happiness was contagious and satisfying as he shared in the reverie,

laughing in delight with the bubbles he could read,

but that was not all he could see.

He was also exposed to the depravity of humankind.

The seven deadly sins were in no short supply,

floating around in the sea of humanity,

on full display for him to observe.

All were unaware of the others' thoughts as they intermingled,

while going about their daily routines.

He could see their thoughts

and unspoken, caustic rejoinders of what they were observing,

unaware of their own lives being viewed with such critical assessment.

If they only knew what opinions walked among them—

    how much people said one thing but thought another;

    how much people pretended to listen while discounting the others;

    how quick people were to pass judgement with what they saw;

    how quickly people could feign care and concern while ulterior motives lurked

        in the recesses of their mind.

But what began to weigh heavily on him,

what caused him pain, was when the bleak side of their soul was laid bare—

    revealing desperation,

    revealing insecurities,

    revealing despondence.

The absolute hopelessness of some was gut-wrenching.

He was a witness to the depression their thoughts divulged,

thoughts he could read but was helpless to alter.

It was during these moments that he resented his power.

It was during these moments that it felt more like a curse.

He couldn't escape what his powers exposed.

Is this, in some small measure, what God deals with?

    the incessant chatter of human thought?

    the aggravation of humankind's selfishness?

    the accumulation of humanity's misery?

It was with him wherever he went—at work, at home, at worship.

It deprived him of relaxation and recreation.

There was only rest with self-imposed isolation,

but the relief was only temporary because his thoughts would eventually turn inward,

leaving him with his own doubts, his own oppressive thought bubbles,

knowing, if they could be read,

would reflect some of the same troubling inclinations in varying degrees.

He was not immune from the vexations of life.

It was like lugging the weight of the world up the side of a mountain,

straining under a load both cumbersome and immense.

What was he to do?

He couldn't stay hidden from the world.

He couldn't spend the remainder of his days sheltered in exile.

The answer: take it one day at a time; deal with it as it comes.

As he eased his way back into his life,

he discovered a new-found empathy for those struggling with their own heavy loads.

He discovered a new desire to help them with their struggle—

    to lift them out of their inner miasma;

    to give them a shoulder upon which to cry;

    to give them a sympathetic listener.

The more he gave, the more he received in return:

    instead of seclusion—fellowship;

    instead of exile—inclusion.

He found he could guide others with his insights

and in turn, teach them how to share the load of others.

It was a learning process for all, an experiment in sharing.

No one person is an Atlas or Sisyphus.

We were intended to share in struggles and ease burdens—
    to experience the joy and happiness of each other;
    to delight in those around us;
    to block out the darkness and let in the light.
Is this, in some small measure, how God feels?

He was just an average guy walking along,
gathering tidbits of information from the thought bubbles
bobbing along above the heads in the stream of people,
no longer cringing from what he saw, no longer shirking his calling.
He was now searching . . . seeking . . .
pursuing those who needed assistance and support . . .
those who needed caring and nurturing.
He no longer considered himself cursed.
He now considered himself . . . blessed.

Note: I was just contemplating what it would be like if this type of power existed and the tremendous weight of responsibility which it would entail on any person who had been given this ability.

WHAT NOW?

If I have it all . . . my heart's desire,
    if all has been accomplished,
    there is nothing left for which to dream.
The journey is over.
I have reached the end.
I look behind to see from where I came—
    to see what was achieved.
I look around and scratch my head.
The celebration at the end feels final.
I have mixed feelings—maybe even bittersweet.
If this is the end, there will never be another such day.

So . . . what do I do now?

Note: What would one do if there was nothing left to work for or achieve? The answer: find something. The alternative: just stop living; run up the white flag and surrender.

MORE THAN A CARD

I watched my wife as she looked thoughtfully . . .
carefully, through her boxes full of well-wishes,
cards contained within for every occasion,
each one meant to bring a glint of sunshine,
meant to brighten the day of those for whom she cared.

The art of card-giving is disappearing,
fast becoming a memory of a bygone time.
No longer is time given to the selection,
is the care given to finding that special card
    to commemorate an occasion,
    to comfort a grieving heart,
    to shout out holiday greetings,
    to just say, "Thinking of you."
The whole process is deemed too "old school",
seeming out of place in this age of technology,
but . . . not to her . . . not to her.
This is her way of extending herself,
of sharing and connecting, though distance separates.

It's been called a ministry of care by her friends.
You see, it's more than the words in the card;
it's the additional notes she inscribes within,
taking the time to pen those special words,
written with sincerity . . .
    meant to sooth and encourage,
    meant to say, "You're not alone,"
    meant to say, "Have faith; better days are just ahead."

I have watched this ministry of hers for years and years.
She seems to know when the card is needed—
an uncanny intuitiveness she has perfected.
What is being received is more than a card.
It's a caring connection, a devotion to friendship . . .
her way of reminding others they are in her thoughts and prayers.

In her quiet, unassuming way, she is touching lives
in ways she may never know,
but her intent is not for praise or adulation.
The giving of the card is a genuine desire
to send hope . . . to send joy . . . to send love.
To her, it will always be more than a card she sends;
It's a message sent from her heart.

Note: This is my tribute to my wife and her special talent and gift when it comes to card-giving. I wrote this as I watched her selecting, writing, and sending her cards to those she felt needed a lift of some kind. I don't know how many times I have heard people express how much the card she sent was such a blessing, that it arrived at just the right moment to offer the encouragement that was so desperately needed. It truly is a ministry of care and love.

THINKING OUT LOUD

The thoughts were pent up, cornered in my mind,
Searching to find a voice on the outside—
A voice yearning to shout to all mankind;
A voice of peace, not one to rant and chide.
But was mankind ready to hear my voice?
My thinking out loud to be heard and tried,
To let composed reason become the choice,
To place anger and malice to the side.
I hope all will join with joyful delight,
Standing together in common respect,
Free from the hindrance of contempt and spite,
Our spirits entwined to care and protect.
    The voice in my head is thinking out loud,
    "Oh, how I want to be part of that crowd."

ABOUT THE AUTHOR

Mike Hall is also the author of another collection of poetry, *Autumn's Back Porch: Reflections of a Life.* He has been a teacher for the past forty-plus years and draws on these experiences to enrich and add humor to his writing.

He and his wife, Cynthia, live in the Dallas area and are the proud parents of three children who have all gone on to marry and have careers of their own. Some of their happiest days are spent with their two grandchildren.

www.ingramcontent.com/pod-product-compliance
Lightning Source LLC
Chambersburg PA
CBHW070445090426
42735CB00012B/2469